Tradition in the Making

The Magic of Handweaving

The Basics and Beyond

Sigrid Piroch

Published by

kp krause publications

An F+W Publications Company

700 East State Street • Iola, WI 54990-0001
715-445-2214 • 888-457-2873
www.krause.com

Our toll-free number to place an order or obtain a free catalog is 800-258-0929.

The front cover photo includes closeups of fabrics woven in Chapter 9: Herringbone Twill, 3/1 and 1/3 twill blocks, and Brighten Honeycomb plus a boat shuttle, pirns, and a color wheel. The title page photo includes these items and an end delivery shuttle.

Library of Congress Catalog Number: 2002107619

ISBN: 0-87349-384-2

Edited by Christine Townsend and Sarah Herman
Designed by Donna Mummery

Printed in the United States of America

Dedication

This book is dedicated with love and thanks to my father, who taught me to view the world through the spectrum of music ... rhythm, melody, and harmony in symphony and opera; to my mother, who taught me to view the world through the spectrum of art ... color, form, and balance in painting and sculpture and—not the least—fibers; and especially to my husband, whose love and support has made all things possible.

Acknowledgments

Little did I know when I called Krause Publications to order some books for my Arts Studio that, before I was off the phone, I would be asked to write one! Here was an opportunity to reach many who might wish to become weavers, to share knowledge studio-tested over three decades with students at all levels of expertise, and to share my enthusiasm for fibers, colors, and weaving. Although I had no intention of writing such a book initially, I couldn't resist the call to action. I am delighted to say that during these past three years, this adventure has posed exciting new challenges and opened doors to work with many others whose lives are dedicated to their love of textiles. I wouldn't have wanted to miss that.

A very special thanks to Bobbie Irwin, weaver *par excellence*, for her exceptional editing skills, support, and friendship. A special commendation to Nancy Lewis who, though arriving "on board" later, created superb illustrations. We are honored to have Paola Gianturco, Toby Tuttle, and Gianni Vecchiato— all world-famous photographers—share their extraordinary gifts of imagery. Thanks especially to Blanche and Bob Hall. You see Blanche throughout the book assisting me with hands and heart, but you don't see the thousand times they both assisted off-camera! A special mention to Merv Stahlman who built our false seven-foot wall for photography and kept all the looms in working order.

Thanks to Halcyon Yarn, Jaggerspun Yarn, Treenway Silks, and Lunatic Fringe for yarn donations; to Schacht Spindle Co. for lending various equipment; to Caphuchi and "Bobbo" Ahiagble for African strip weaving; to Licia Conforti and Meg Stump for small looms; to Maureen Dow at Cedar Hollow, Barbara Borgerd at Gentle Wovens, and Carol Leigh of Hillcreek Studio, for documentation and photographs of triangle weaving; to the Yarn Barn in Lawrence, Kansas, for textile videos; to these folks: Karen Selk, Gudrun Weisinger, Judy Hanninen, Sarah Nantani, Dana McCown, Kathleen

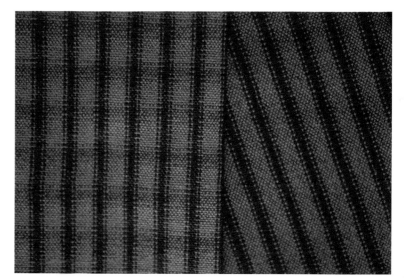

Johnson, Deb McClintock, Kati Meek, Judie Eatough, and Enid Allen, Senior Visual Products Specialist for Munsell®.

Thank you also to J.M. Adovasio, Ph.D., D.Sc. (Professor, Anthropology, Archaeology, and Geology and Director of the Science Division and Mercyhurst Archaeological Institute) and J.S. Illingworth (Director of Curation and Conservation, Supervisor R.L. Anderws Center for Perishables Analysis) at Mercyhurst Archaeological Institute in Erie, Pennsylvania, for their archaeological assistance. Thanks to the staff of non-profit museums. Please use and support these excellent facilities: the Alling Coverlet Museum in Palmyra, New York; Home Textile Tool Museum in Rome, Pennsylvania; Shelburne Museum in Connecticut; Ontario Science Centre in Toronto, Ontario, Canada; Jefferson County Historical Society in Watertown, New York; Handweaving Museum & Arts Center in Clayton, New York.; and the American Textile History Museum in Lowell, Massachusetts. Please also support cottage industries throughout the world, such as *Studio Naenna*, Chiang Mai, Thailand, and *Lao Textiles*, Vientiane, Laos, as they depend on us for their very survival. And thanks without measure to my wonderful husband, who kept the household running (and us both well fed) while I focused on this book.

Contents

Foreword

Once in a while a new book on weaving appears that takes an old subject and presents it in such a dramatic, new way that every weaver and everyone who hopes to be a weaver will feel that they must have it in their libraries. This book is just such a book.

The art and skill of weaving is certainly not an invention of the twenty-first century, or of the fourteenth century, or of the first century. Weaving was practiced 26,000 years ago. Human beings found it useful then, and humans the world over could not live without it today. The form and appearance of woven pieces vary in different countries and in different cultures, but basically weaving is an art in which one thread, or straw, or wire, etc., is interlaced with another to form a useful or decorative piece. That sounds remarkably simple, but weaving can take so many forms that it can also be remarkably complex. The author of this book has taken the complexity out of the process by describing it in such clear terms that one can teach oneself to weave simple, and then progressively more complicated, fabrics. Sigrid Piroch is eminently qualified for such a task. She is a talented, well-known weaver and weaving teacher who has inspired many people to start weaving, and many more to continue to become excellent weavers. She has done this through hundreds of workshops and lectures over the past 30 years in the United States, Canada, Australia/Tasmania, New Zealand, Sweden, Germany, Slovakia, Thailand, and Laos. The many magazine articles she has written have graced the pages of essentially all the prominent weaving magazines in the United States, Canada, and Australia.

The reader will find the processes in this book written with the clear and easy-to-follow instructions for which the author is known. Both new and experienced weavers will be enticed by the step-by-step processes, and by more than 300 color photographs and illustrations of weaving equipment and woven fabrics. The author has used the very valuable technique of making a chapter into one or more lessons. These chapters end with one or more projects that embody the salient parts of those lessons and that includes all of the details the weaver needs in order to weave a useful or decorative piece. Color photos and drawings illustrate each lesson. Each chapter builds on the previous one so the student learns, and puts into practice, a new skill. Subsequent chapters with weaving projects and photos add to the student's excitement about weaving *and* to the honing of his/her weaving skills. Thus this book lays the foundation for an art/craft that can grow with each chapter, and that can be the weaver's jumping-off point for many years of pleasure in creating something both useful and beautiful.

By creating this handsomely illustrated, clearly written instructional book, the author has performed a valuable service for both weaver and non-weaver alike. Beginners will find excellent instructions for learning to weave. More experienced weavers will find useful review and study materials. All will find challenge in the lessons of fabric analysis, as well as in planning and weaving projects for a loom of up to eight shafts. The curious reader, who just wants to know how cloth is made and how designs are created, will appreciate the how-to photos, the equipment, and the fabrics.

Helen N. Jarvis

Helen Jarvis is a long-time handweaver who uses many different techniques in her weaving, but has made the reproduction of early American bed coverings, called coverlets, her specialty. Some of her coverlets can be found in museum villages and historic houses. She has taught many hundreds of weavers in the United States and Canada to weave coverlets, and wrote *Weaving a Traditional Coverlet*, the definitive work on the process.

Introduction:
The Magic of Handweaving

I still remember when I first began to weave ... there was a new vocabulary to get accustomed to, new equipment to learn to use, and new yarns about which to learn. It came in bits and pieces and got put together in bits and pieces, but was never difficult because there was always someone near to assist, to care, and to share. I delighted in the many books on weaving I found, each of which brought some new thinking to the creative process. Today guilds, conferences, and the Internet bring friends even closer with information, support, and answers. It will come about for you, too, and my hope is that this book becomes one of your companions on your journey.

As I write this, I think back on the years of weaving that are certainly not just threads, but the people who made it happen. I see the brass reed hook shown in Chapter 2 and recall how my son Joey, then age 7, wrote his first real letter to order one for me that Christmas. It has been in constant use for over 25 years. I see the looms in Chapter 3 and am reminded of my first big loom, a surprise present from the whole family another Christmas, hidden in a friend's truck for a week in our driveway. The tree in the front yard is where my daughter posed bravely for photos in my first hand-woven garments, even though the neighbors were watching. Each time I weave on my inkle loom, as in Chapter 1, I am aware of the sense of belonging I felt with friends eager to assist this new weaver at my first guild meetings in Chautauqua, New York. Every time I make a weaver's cross, as in Chapter 5, I see the smile of the lovely lady who first showed me how when I bought my first warping board. My weaving instructors have each brought something special as they supported me in my development, broadening my vision. Still, I may have learned the most by my mistakes that I tell myself are only detours on the way to achieving that desired end. And I have my students to thank for challenging me almost daily.

I try never to lose sight of the traditions that have come down to us from generations of weavers before us. Working out of this store of knowledge has gradually helped me realize how I cherish the entire process of creating. I become part of it as it becomes part of me. There is the excitement of discovery from the first inkling of an idea through to developing the design to the finished weaving. In fact, I can't think of anything about weaving that I don't like. But it's the people who make it the most special, those who came before to lay the foundation, those here now who share the adventure, and those just beginning to discover the *magic*.

Photo courtesy of Simplicity Pattern Co., Inc.

Tradition in the Making

Traditions of weaving throughout the world challenge us to appreciate their great diversity.

Weaving beckons us from its frontiers, lost in the mists of time, whispering of its mysteries. The history of handweaving is the history of mankind. It is the story of man's intimate relationship with his environment and his creative utilization of those resources for survival. The history of weaving takes us back to the earliest days of man's existence, but, since textiles are perishable, much has been lost in the vestiges of time. Yet direct evidence and artistic representations take us back at least 26,000 years.

Today, cloth is so "everyday" we take it for granted. It is no longer a requirement of everyday life to help in the production of cloth, so we approach the process with renewed wonder. Some methods are simple enough for a youngster to learn quickly, and some, in times past, so complex a whole echelon of society was enlisted for production, sometimes evolving over centuries. It's no wonder we can "forever" study the many and varied aspects of handweaving, always exciting and new.

Until the Industrial Revolution, to create cloth, one had to sort out what to use for thread, how to acquire it, a means to spin it, and then a way to weave it. Until 1856, when Sir Henry Perkins discovered aniline dyes, natural dyes were the only means to color fibers. With so much effort, no wonder every available piece of cloth was precious, nothing was wasted of it, and patterns for clothing were designed so every piece was put to use. Today, we are familiar with recycling scraps of cloth into quilts and rag rugs. Though cloth was known to be perishable, weavers still went to great pains to make textiles as beautiful as possible. Then, just as now, cloth was used to enhance both the wearer and the environment. The word "heir-loom" means just that ... looms are durable and a good investment because they lead very long lives, often over generations. When I weave on one of my antique looms, I feel myself touching back to those who wove before me. Such traditions are, for us, the steppingstones for today and tomorrow ... *tradition in the making*.

The Basics of Handweaving

If you are a new weaver, or a weaver-to-be, it is my pleasure to introduce you to handweaving. Or perhaps you wish to review "the basics" and firm up your skills. Join me as we take a closer look at what is needed to get started weaving, the equipment used, and the classic methods by which it is done. Learn the language of weaving through bolded terms that I later define. Explore some looms that are small, portable, and inexpensive. Move step-by-step through the process of setting up a table and floor loom, designing and warping to weave various projects—rag place mats, mug rugs, scarves, pillows, towels, runners, color samplers, vests, and more. Decide whether new or used equipment is best for you. Learn to read drafts and do drawdowns. Learn to analyze a textile, generate the draft, and weave it again. Much about weaving can be learned quickly. We'll take it a step at a time, a chapter at a time.

Scattered throughout the book are weavers around the world whose weaving is their daily work, together with historic references. I also scatter a showcase of fabric treasures by some of the finest weavers today throughout the pages—inspiration at its best, *tradition in the making*. Check my Web site at www.artsstudio.org for resources that complement each topic by chapter: books, bibliographies, suppliers, organizations, other Web sites, and much more.

As you read this book, you will feel the *magic* when you throw your first shuttle and see the *magic* when, even on a plain warp, shapes and colors and patterns emerge as if out of nowhere. Weaving is craft and art that merge as one. It is structure and color working together. Weaving crosses cultures with distinction. It knows no boundaries, no language impediments, and no religious or social barriers. Discover the wonder, let your imagination soar— weave your dreams.

Small, Simple, Portable Looms

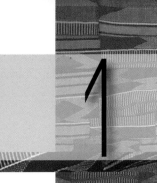

Band ends require finishing, which can be done in many ways: Shown are various methods of fingerweaving by Ernestine Sample. Today, Kumihimo (plaited cords) and other Japanese braids are very popular, along with Peruvian methods.

Using 4-hole tablets, Ernestine Sample weaves these belts, and by sewing a number together, creates a purse of bands.

Catch the *magic*. Small looms are portable and an excellent introduction to handweaving. Simple to learn and use, they come in a variety of sizes and types, are easily transported, and most are inexpensive. You may want to get the "feel" of weaving by trying out such a loom. These encourage creativity with yarns, color, and structure as you become acquainted with how cloth is made. Such equipment can help orient you to weaving and weaving terms, help you decide what you like to weave, and consider features most important to you in that bigger loom you are dreaming of. Yet each of these methods of weaving offers challenges to take you to a new level of interest, because *the simpler the loom, the more flexible its capacity for design*. Thus these looms also captivate experienced weavers. Many of these looms come with instructions.

Small Hand Looms

Remember those little potholder looms? As kids, many of us wove squares on them with loops cut from old socks, T-shirt sleeves, or packaged loopers. Weave these in and out each direction; teeth along the sides hold the end loops until weaving is finished, ready to slip them off. Potholder looms are still available.

My mother wove small squares with me on a little loom called a Weave-It, a yarn equivalent. Now called Weavette™, these looms are made of hardwood with stainless steel pins, small enough to hold in your hand. Create cloth by weaving yarns with a long needle over and under other yarns stretched on the loom. Experiment with assorted types and colors. Assemble these small squares into larger shapes for clothing, toys, and other items. The smallest square now made is two inches, the ultimate in weaving portability.

Blanche Hall uses Weavette looms, the 1945 Weave-It book, and Licia Conforti's book, Textured Patterns for the Weavette Loom, *to make various experimental design squares in wool, cotton, novelty, and other yarns.*

Six sizes of triangle looms from Gentle Wovens.

Triangle Looms

The triangle loom concept is thought to have developed in the 1400s in Great Britain. This type of weaving has become very popular. Several methods of weaving have been developed, so you may want to try more than one. You can weave on a loom in a triangle shape that is less than 18 inches across or up to seven feet across.

To weave a triangle,

only one continuous strand of yarn is used for the entire weaving. Each round is the same length even though a triangle is not the same length on each side. Most are woven as a balanced plain weave, the same number of threads in each direction, but you can also do fancier weaving such as lace, diagonal twills, even two layers (double-weave).

Use woven triangles "as is," sewn in pairs to make squares, or assemble to create other forms. Triangles in one or more sizes can be pieced for caps, baby buntings, collars, scarves, vests, sweaters, jackets, ruanas, purses, blankets, and afghans, to name a few. Weavings are creative. You can make a poncho assembled with anywhere from eight to 48 triangles or a bath mat to fit a tub corner.

Color plays an important part in how the woven triangle will look. Plaids are popular. So is a method using space-dyed yarns to create "sunset shawls," designed so each corner is a solid color and the center colors blend. You'll find exciting examples on Web sites and in triangle chat room libraries.

Sunset Triangle Shawl by Barbara Borgerd.

Weaving by Blanche Hall on a rigid heddle loom.

Design detail of a weaving by Blanche Hall on a rigid heddle loom, showing the slot-and-hole beater-reed.

Rigid Heddle Looms

These looms are found in most cultures and have a long history. They may be very narrow for weaving bands, sometimes cut from one piece of wood; or wide, with more supporting pieces. This loom is often called a "slot-and-hole" loom because it has vertical sticks, each with a hole in the center, spaced apart by slots. (These resemble frozen treat sticks with holes in the centers, sitting side-by-side with a little space between each.) When the loom (if small) or the frame in the loom (if larger) is raised or lowered, the threads in the holes move up or down while those in each slot stay put. These motions create an opening (shed) between the top and bottom threads, through which you insert the weft yarn. The frame also serves as a beater to pack in the weft, making cloth.

Band Weaving

Bands are quite ancient, from every culture. A band is a long, narrow weaving used for belts, bindings, animal halters, and trim. They have an incredible number of practical and decorative uses, even as shoelaces and earrings. It's a good bet that bands were among the first weavings ever made. One way to weave bands is on an inkle loom; examples of bands made using tablets or cards follow. These are typically warp-faced; warp yarns are so close together, weft shows only at the edges.

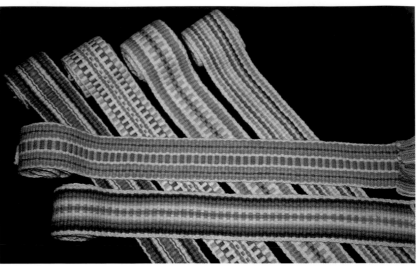

Inkle bands of natural-dyed wools by Sigrid Piroch.

Inkle Loom

An inkle loom is a simple apparatus designed just to weave bands. Easy to set up, they are portable fun for all. Weaving with different colors in two sheds is standard, but interesting variations can include different yarns, patterns, and textures. Directions should come with a new loom.

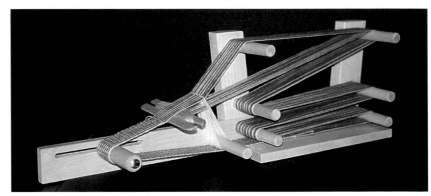

Inkle loom set up and weaving (Schacht Spindle Co.).

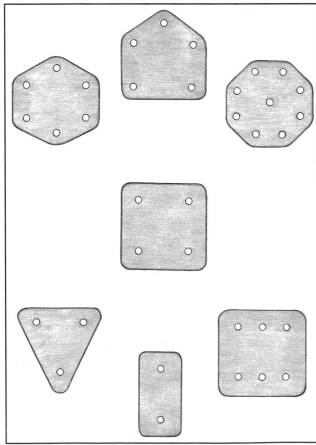

Tablets for weaving.

Tablet Weaving

Tablet weaving (also known as card weaving) requires only a set of tablets (or cards) and some yarns. Historically, these tablets were made of thin, sturdy material: leather, bronze, ivory, bone, wood, stone, horn, pottery, or clay. The most common tablets today are cardboard squares with a hole near each corner, but tablets may have different shapes and different numbers of holes.

The number of tablets used at one time is generally limited by how many a weaver can hold and turn at one time. Typically, yarns are threaded through holes in tablets that are placed in a stack. Yarns at one end are hooked to something to stabilize them (anything from a tree to a doorknob) and those at the other end are attached to the weaver's belt. This is the loom. The order of colors and direction of tablet turnings (the standard is four forward and four back) creates the patterning. These four turnings/sheds are the equivalent of a 4-shaft loom-in-hand, but with extra twist for additional strength.

Tapestry Weaving

Tapestry weaving is one of the oldest of all art forms, tracing back to Babylon, Persia, Egypt, India, and even ancient Greece—tapestries were found on the Parthenon walls. Not only did tapestries enrich and enhance the environment and add warmth to castle walls, but they recorded myths and historic events as well. Tapestry has also been used on a small scale to decorate clothing, such as fifth and sixth century Coptic examples from Egypt. Ideal for weaving pictorial and geometric designs, tapestry weaving is evident in all its forms around the world today.

Most tapestry weavers use a vertical loom, from hand-held to tabletop to floor models to room size. However, you can use any loom if the warp is set wide enough since tapestry is weft-faced, the weft completely covering the warp.

Tiny tapestry in progress by Ernestine Sample on a simple cardboard loom.

Above, a simple yet functional tapestry loom from Harrisville Designs weaving three different tapestries at once. A cartoon behind the center weaving is the weaver's guide to placement and design.

Below, "Sundance at Sea" tapestry by Sigrid Piroch.

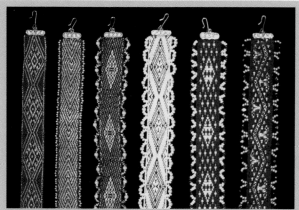

Inge Dam weaves reconstructed bands based on extensive research into surviving ancient examples. These include bands inspired by textiles from the Iron Age (500 BC - AD 800) and the Viking Period (AD 800 - 1050), here made into bracelets embellished with silk, silver, and gold. The history of tablet woven bands is fascinating. Actual bands and yarns rarely survive antiquity. The earliest direct evidence of tablet weaving dates from 400 BC with tablets found in a cave in Spain.

These ten belts and two purses by John Dewdney use mostly 6-hole tablets and irregular turnings.

Two tablet-woven bands of linen by Peter Collingwood, each begun with a round (tubular) starting loop: "AlphaBelt" (top) and "Do it yourself – don't reLION others" with the lion woven in 3/1 broken twill.

Weaving with beads in its various forms is quite popular today, whether hand-held or using one of the many types of bead looms, horizontal or vertical, that hold wire under tension. To weave irregular shapes, you can use pins on a board. Right, a necklace in process by Joanna McDermot, #19 from the Fitzgerald and Banes' book, Beads and Threads, together with two other necklaces inspired by this book: Small beaded necklace by Carmen F. Osborne (top center) and beaded bracelet from high in the Andes Mountains (upper right) from the collection of Jill Rouke.

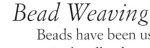

Beads can be culturally important. This Ndebele mother in South Africa is wearing 15-foot beaded panels called "long tears"; she is in ritual mourning because her son has reached the age where he will never use his childhood name again.

Photo by Paola Gianturco and Toby Tuttle.

Bead Weaving

Beads have been used throughout the centuries by all cultures as decoration for people, animals, environment, for trade and dowries, even prayer and *magic*. We can trace bead weaving to sites in France over 38,000 years ago. Beads come in an astounding array of shapes, sizes, and patterns made of glass, clay, semiprecious stones, and gems, all manner of metal including silver and gold, pearls, seashells, tortoise shell, antlers, seeds, paper, bamboo, ivory, even teeth and snake vertebrae.

African Strip Weaving

In some parts of West Africa, large textiles are created by sewing together many strips woven on narrow handlooms, some embellished with decorative threads. Gilbert "Bobbo" Ahiagble is a traditional Kente cloth weaver in Ghana. His ancestors have been weavers for generations and he is teaching his sons to be weavers. His Ewe cloth is "talking cloth" that teaches their culture and history through stories and proverbs that become symbolic pictures in the weavings. For example, one pattern is called "Afetorgbor," which literally means, "the old people are settled," but is interpreted to mean "they have their freedom." Colors are also symbolic.

You can learn from Bobbo at the *Craft Institute of Kente Weaving* in his village of Denu on the south coast of West Africa. The villagers say "the world is a loom that holds countless threads" and their lives "are woven together like threads on the loom."

Bobbo demonstrates weaving in native dress on his loom with a double set of frames. He uses coconut shells for the pedals since he lives in a coconut grove.

Weavers around the World

In southern Mexico and Central America, Maya women weave colorful clothing such as skirts and huipils for their family's needs. The huipil is a simple blouse, cut in the shape of a cross—at its center, natural and supernatural worlds meet. Into these garments the weaver puts patterns from her culture, symbolic of myths and dreams. She chooses motifs that express her complex view of the universe. In it, the sun and moon rotate through day and night, through time and space, with stars the crowns of saints. A weaving can tell folktales, centuries old, resplendent with images of ancestors and earthlords, birds and animals, lightning and floods, trees and flowers. Each weaver's brocaded designs are expressed in original ways.

Photo by Paola Gianturco and Toby Tuttle.

A weaver in Sumpango, Guatemala, wears a lovely huipil as she weaves lightning-like patterns into her weaving on a backstrap loom made of but a few sticks and strands of yarn.

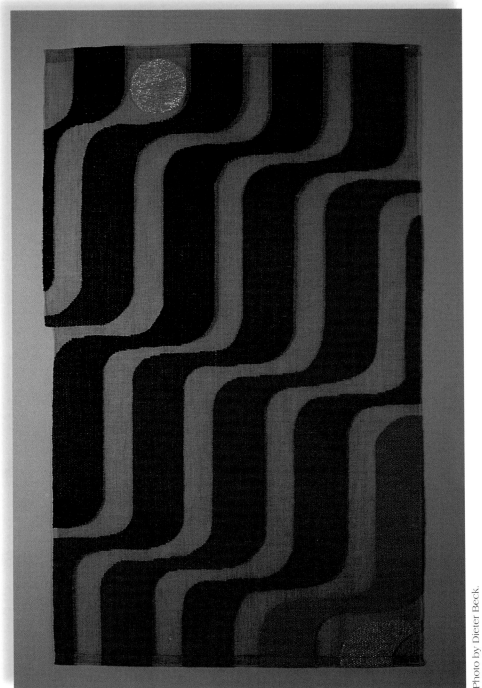

Ulrike Beck's
"Cascading Colors,"
transparency, 38"
wide x 61½" long.

Photo by Dieter Beck.

The first time I wove on a loom there was a magic I will never forget as patterns and colors seemed to appear out of nowhere. I relive that moment with a special joy every time I begin a new project, more than 25 years later.

What is weaving? What is a loom and what are its parts? To communicate with one another, we need to use some weaving terms. Before we answer the question, "what is weaving?," first we must ask "what is cloth?"

Cloth is a fabric or textile. We are surrounded by cloth. It is so much a part of our everyday lives that we tend to take it for granted. We wear it, we sleep on it, we eat on it, we sit on it, we use it in our homes, and we decorate with it. How different life would be without cloth. From hankies to high-fashion clothing, for each of us, cloth is essential.

Not all cloth is woven, so what is woven cloth? Some cloth is felted, knitted, crocheted, twined, or otherwise constructed of fibers or filaments, natural or artificial. Visualize woven cloth as a set of threads or yarns laid flat, interlaced with another set of threads or yarns at a right angle. A **loom** is a device that holds one set of threads under tension (called **warp**) while it is crossed at a right angle with another set (called **weft**). A **shuttle** or other tool carries the weft across. A loom has a shedding device to separate some tensioned threads from others by lifting and/or dropping them so the shuttle, with its weft, can be sent through that **shed**. And, finally, the weaver or the loom will have some means to **beat** each weft thread into place, one at a time. The result is woven cloth.

For many centuries, all cloth was woven of natural fibers that were first drawn out and twisted into thread by a handspinner, during a process called **handspinning**. Today, some cloth is woven in a textile mill using automated machinery and some is woven by hand on a handloom. **Handweaving** is the process of placing threads under tension on a loom and weaving in other threads by hand rather than by machine, usually using a hand shuttle. Cloth today can still be handwoven of handspun fibers from plants and animals, such as cotton and wool and flax that becomes linen thread, or cloth can be handwoven of mill yarns.

In the late 1800s, mills were developed that put to use the large, newly invented, automated metal looms that produced cloth quickly and without a weaver. Mill cloth today comes in a wide variety of fibers, structures, colors, and patterns. However, since the intent of a mill is to make as much cloth as it can sell commercially, a mill never makes one-of-a-kind pieces. Handweavers, on the other hand, have control over the entire process of making handwoven cloth, which includes selection of type, size, and color of threads, how these interlace, and whether it is for an art or functional purpose.

Handweaving produces any type of fabric, from very heavy items, such as rugs and coatings, to medium-weight fabrics for vests and place mats, to light-weight fabrics for blouses and tablecloths, to very delicate fabrics for sheer curtains, to the latest high-tech fabrics. So, handweaving can be practical or decorative, or both.

Most handweavers prefer to weave with natural fibers and most handlooms are still made of wood. Today, thread is still handspun and cloth is still handwoven for everyday use around the world, mostly in third world countries, to provide for their essential needs, as well as for decoration. Over the last century in countries that utilize mill cloth extensively, such as ours, handspinning and handweaving have evolved to include the creation of special threads and specialized fabrics. We in America have drawn from these established traditions of knowledge and skill to make up our own unique textile heritage, and still we continue to grow and evolve in new ways—*tradition in the making.*

The gray vertical threads are warp and the blue horizontal threads are weft.

Basic Weaving Terms

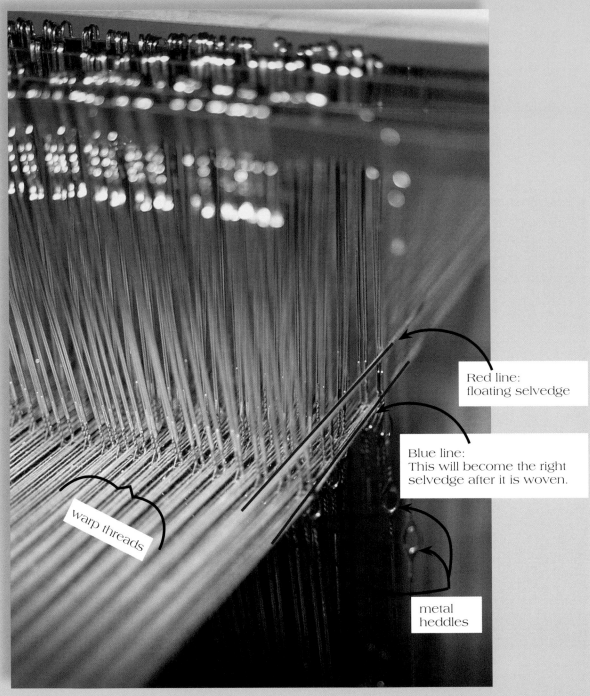

Red line:
floating selvedge

Blue line:
This will become the right
selvedge after it is woven.

warp threads

metal
heddles

Detail of a floating selvedge, warp threads, and heddles on a loom.

While it's not necessary to commit the following definitions to memory, reading through them will help you become familiar with these terms as you proceed.

A **weaving** is a textile made up of one set of elements (known as warps) that is interlaced at a right angle with another set (known as wefts). These elements are generally threads or yarns. In a simple textile, such as those in this book, there is one set of each at work; in a complex or compound textile, there are two or more warp and/or weft sets; there may also be two or more layers, usually somehow integrated.

Warp is a set of vertical or lengthwise elements

in a textile that run parallel to each other and at a right angle to the weft. A single thread of warp is called an **end**. **Ends per inch** (epi) is the number of warp ends in one inch, also called **sett** (example: the sett is 12 epi). (See **Sett Chart** on page 43.)

Weft is a set of horizontal or widthwise elements in a textile that run parallel to each other and at a right angle to the warp. A single thread of weft is called a **pick**. **Picks per inch** (ppi) is the number of weft picks in one inch. (Museums and countries often use the decimal system and describe warp and weft spacing in centimeters, i.e., epc and ppc.)

Thread and **yarn** are terms that can be used interchangeably; thread sometimes implies a finer size and yarn sometimes implies a heavier size.

Face is the topside of the fabric on the loom; back is the underside.

The warping process is the method by which threads are counted as they are measured all the same length, rolled onto the loom, and tensioned, ready to weave.

The process of weaving is the method by which warp and weft threads are interlaced to construct a textile.

A **shed** is a v-shaped opening in the warp threads created by lifting and/or dropping some of those threads for the purpose of entering the weft.

A **selvedge** is the woven edge of a weaving.

A **floating selvedge** is an extra thread added at the edge of a warp for

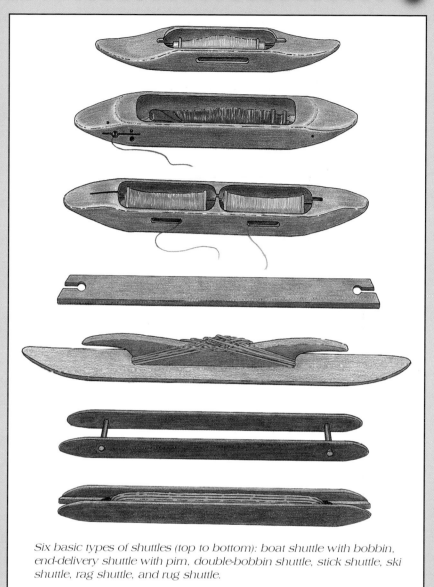

Six basic types of shuttles (top to bottom): boat shuttle with bobbin, end-delivery shuttle with pirn, double-bobbin shuttle, stick shuttle, ski shuttle, rag shuttle, and rug shuttle.

certain weaves, such as twills, to catch the weft right at the selvedge each time. It is only needed when the weft would otherwise skip in and out along the edge. It is threaded through a reed dent, but not through a heddle. This thread "floats" in the center of every shed, neither up nor down. The shuttle is thrown *over* the float and automatically comes out *under* the float at the other side.

A **shuttle** is a device, usually of wood, that carries the weft through the shed.

 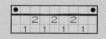

Floating selvedges are shown as dots at the ends of a threading draft, such as in these two examples of plain weave drafts with seven threads and two floating selvedges.

WEAVERS AROUND THE WORLD

Backstrap weaving is ancient and still used in many cultures. One end of a set of threads is tied to a stick that, in turn, is tied to a stable object such as a tree. The other end is tied to a stick and fastened to a strap around the weaver. This back strap, when she leans back, puts tension on the threads. In between are cords to keep threads in order and sticks to lift them.

Olivia Asij, a weaver in Santo Domingo Xenacoj, Guatemala, weaves colorful stripes.

Photo by Paola Gianturco and Toby Tuttle.

Looms

There is an interesting maxim in handweaving: The simpler the loom, the more versatile it is. Any weaving structure, in any color combination, can be woven on a simple loom, sometimes using simple tools to pick up and drop certain threads as they are woven in. While it is possible to weave complex patterns and fabrics using simple equipment, by far the easiest way to produce most weavings quickly and practically is with looms like those described in this book. The ability of such looms to weave a wide range of fabrics, something most weavers today desire, explains their popularity. No longer are we subject to cultural expectations or necessities of times past, though we should still utilize our historic resources. We have these men and women weavers to thank for their genius in adapting and refining looms over many centuries of use so they operate at maximum efficiency. Looms vary some by locality and manufacturer, but the basic parts of a loom and their mechanics are the same.

Looms produce handwoven samples and projects on a small scale as well as the production weaving of multiple items and yardage on a larger scale. Looms come in different sizes and widths for different purposes, from smaller table looms to larger floor looms. Some floor looms of the eighteenth and nineteenth centuries, often called "barn looms" in America, were made of huge wooden beams on which coverlets and household linens were woven—some of these are still weaving today. Floor looms made today come in a wide variety of sizes and features, from compact workshop looms to heavy rug looms, and many models in-between. Projects in this book are woven on a table loom, and later on a floor loom, but can be woven on either.

Whether you have a loom from your grandmother's attic, have found one at an auction, are building one, or are buying one new, this book will get you weaving. Not only are used looms available to buy, but new looms are affordable if you compare prices, for example, to a new sewing machine. Many handweaving guilds throughout America and other countries have looms and equipment to lease at low costs. The Handweavers Guild of America (HGA), a national organization, has many resources of its own and can help you contact learning centers and guilds in your area. The Internet is also an excellent source for the latest in equipment and supplies; chat lists encourage questions and discussion.

Looms are a good investment because a good loom will not wear out except over generations, which also means it is possible to resell it, often for at least the price you paid for it. The word *heirloom* says it all.

Essential Parts of a Loom

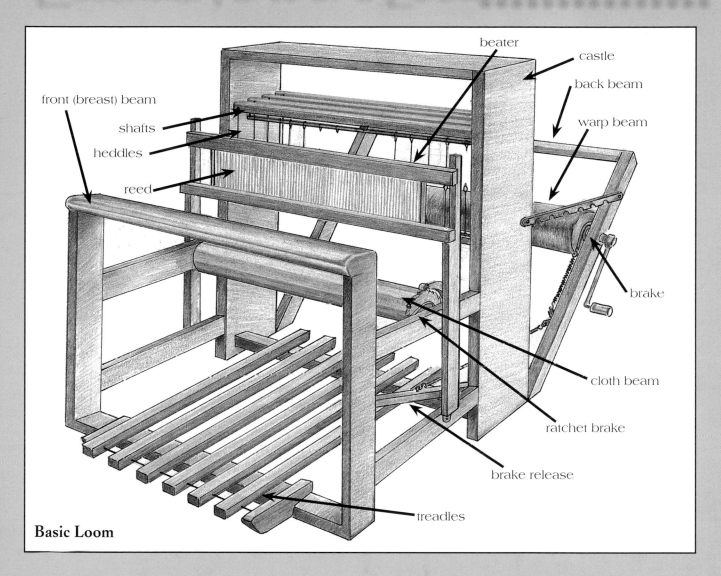

beater

castle

back beam

warp beam

front (breast) beam

shafts

heddles

reed

brake

cloth beam

ratchet brake

brake release

treadles

Basic Loom

Basic Floor Loom: Here is the structure of a 4-shaft handloom with six treadles, labeled with parts found on most looms. Additional working parts, the mechanisms in the middle of a loom that are unique to each of the three basic loom types, are shown and labeled later in this chapter.

A **shaft** is a frame, the shedding device on a loom. (The common use of *harness* in the past, applied to these looms, is inaccurate.) Shafts in America are numbered from nearest the weaver (one) to X (the total number of shafts on the loom) at the back. A loom must have at least two shafts to create a shed. Rug looms often have just two shafts. Pattern looms have four or more shafts. Eight-shaft looms are recommended for most modern weaving, making it possible to weave every project in this book ... and a whole lot more. "Thinking 8-shafts" will take you on a long and exciting journey.

A **heddle** is a length of string or metal attached to the top and bottom of a shaft. A heddle has an "eye" at the center through which a warp end is threaded. The warp is normally threaded in sequence for a design, one end per heddle on two or more shafts. When one or more shafts lift and/or drop, a v-shaped shed is created, with some threads above and some threads below, through which the shuttle is thrown.

Hint

Heddles come with each group tied all the same direction. Use string through the top and bottom loops to slide them onto each shaft so that they don't become mixed up: right and left, up and down, or top and bottom.

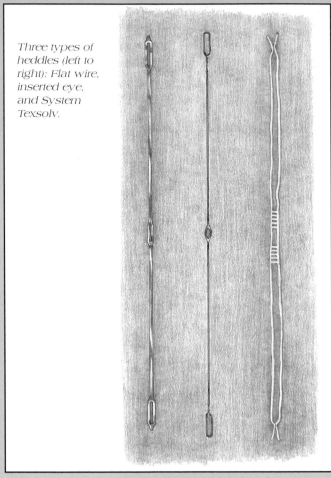

Three types of heddles (left to right): Flat wire, inserted eye, and System Texsolv.

so the weft thread is *between* some warp threads above and some below, then beaten into place. It is not just the size, type, and color of warp and weft threads that creates textures and patterns in cloth, but also the order in which the warp is threaded on the loom. Each group of shafts with its set of heddles offers tremendous potential for variations in structure, because any warp thread at any point in the weaving can be threaded on any one of them. The more shafts on a loom, the more pattern combinations become possible. Furthermore, after the loom is threaded, you can operate one or more shafts at a time. The combinations in which these shafts are used, and the order in which they weave, make texture and pattern possibilities essentially unlimited.

The **beater** is a long, rectangular frame housing the reed. It sits between the shafts and front beam; the top can be removed to change the reed. Its

A sliding beater is my favorite, shown on AVL's Studio Dobby Loom.

Heddles come in a variety of heights for different looms. If you have a used loom with string heddles, I encourage you to replace them. Twisted wire heddles are the least costly, followed by flat steel with a hole punched at the center. An inserted-eye heddle with its round, smooth eye may be easier on threads and more likely to withstand heavy use. The eye on most modern metal heddles is slanted so you can set them up all slanted to the right or to the left, depending on whether you are right-handed or left-handed, and whether you warp front-to-back or back-to-front. Many heddles are also color-coded on top so you can more easily keep the entire bunch upright on each shaft.

Textures and Patterns: As the weft skips over or under more than one thread across, and as it repeats this skipping in various combinations from one shed to the next, textures and/or patterns develop as the cloth is being woven. Since the weft is sent *through* a shed, how do threads skip over and/or under?

Each warp thread is in a specific heddle on a specific shaft. When a shaft is lifted or dropped, a shed is created through which the shuttle is thrown, function is to pack the weft. The beater moves forward and back as it pivots from its anchor point at the bottom of a loom, hung overhead on a frame, or sliding on steel rods at the side. A sliding beater comes closest to the ideal of the beater hitting the cloth at a perfect right angle of 90 degrees. Another beater can also produce excellent results if it hits at close to this angle, and if the warp is advanced at frequent intervals of one inch to two inches.

A reed in a beater shows the warp threaded through it, the fell line of the woven cloth, and the cloth selvedges.

Shaft looms have a **reed,** which sits in the beater. A reed has vertical metal teeth held together at even intervals in a frame. Each space in a reed is a **dent**. Warp threads are spaced across through dents, usually one or more threads per dent. Reeds come in various sizes based on the number of dents per inch, such as 10 dents per inch (10 dpi reed). Most weavers have several reeds for various sett possibilities. Reeds are made the weaving width of the loom—a warp is centered in it. Originally, reeds were made of real reed, but today they are made of either carbon or stainless steel. Stainless reeds cost a little more, but are more practical in humid areas since carbon reeds may rust or pit.

To **sley** is to put a warp thread through a dent in the reed. To **thread** is to put a warp thread through a heddle on a shaft. The **fell line** of the cloth is the woven edge where the last pick was beaten in.

The Three Basic Loom Types

Most weavers use one or more of these three types of handlooms: Jack, countermarch, and counterbalance. Each differs primarily in how the shafts create a shed by moving up and/or down and/or remain at rest at any given time.

With a **jack loom**, some shafts *rise* while others remain *at rest.* (The focus is on *one or more shafts rising.*)

With a **countermarch loom**, when some shafts *rise,* all other shafts *drop.* (The focus is on *all shafts active*, rising or dropping.)

With a **counterbalance loom**, all shafts work in pairs; when one of a pair *drops,* the other of that pair *rises* to balance it. (The focus is *one or more shafts dropping.*)

If you have a **jack loom** or plan to get one, especially if you are new to weaving, you may wish to focus just on the information below. A **counterbalance loom**, in addition to being available new, is often found for sale as a used loom and much of our weaving heritage comes out of that tradition, so if you are a jack loom weaver, this information may become important for you. If you are planning to obtain a new or used loom, compare features of all three types to see what is right for you. Whatever loom type and size you have or plan to get, this book will get you weaving on it.

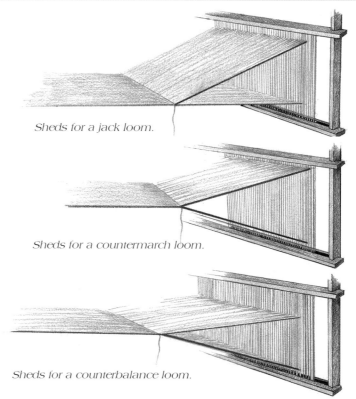

Sheds for a jack loom.

Sheds for a countermarch loom.

Sheds for a counterbalance loom.

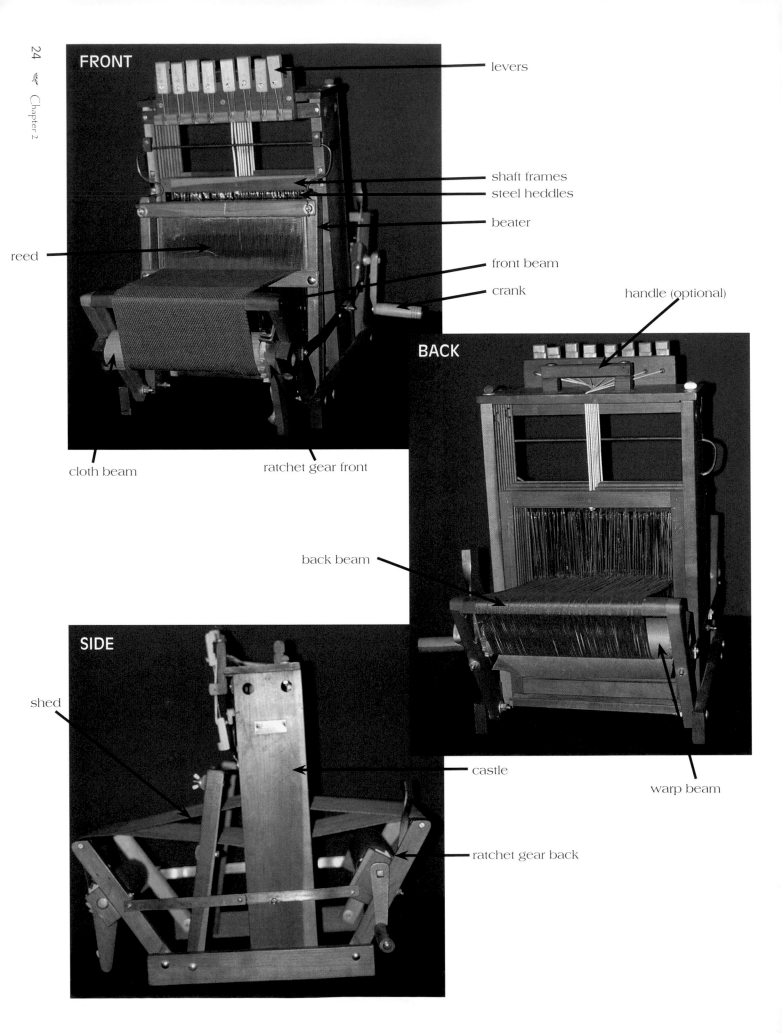

FRONT

levers

shaft frames

steel heddles

beater

reed

front beam

crank

handle (optional)

cloth beam

ratchet gear front

BACK

back beam

SIDE

shed

castle

warp beam

ratchet gear back

Table Looms

Most table looms are jack looms, activated by pulling down a lever on the front (shown in the side view), side, or top, which lifts one or more shafts. The table loom pictured has shafts that move up and down in slots in the sides. Two advantages of a table loom are its small size and portability. Although a table loom is a handy, flexible design tool to try out different yarns and shed combinations, you cannot get a weaving rhythm going on it as you can on a floor loom because the levers are changed by hand. Many weavers use a table loom for sampling and small projects, and a floor loom to weave larger projects.

Floor Looms

Floor looms have foot **treadles**; long, narrow, wooden slats secured under the loom front to back, each connected to one or more shafts. When each treadle is tied directly to a single shaft, this is called a **direct tie-up**. However, when using this method, especially on a wide loom with a narrow warp, shafts may not remain level when weaving. To better stabilize the shafts, most floor looms have a set of **lamms** located between the shafts and treadles. Lamms are a set of sticks that run side to side, each approximately the length and width of a shaft, tied to

treadles *below* as well as to one or more shafts *above*. When a treadle is connected to more than one shaft at a time by this method, it is called a **multiple-shaft tie-up**.

Usually a floor loom has two more treadles than the number of shafts; historically, two are tied to weave the fabric background and the others to weave the fabric pattern. Treadles can be mounted under the loom and hinged (1) at the front, (2) at the rear, or, more rarely (3) a combination of both. Many weavers prefer the first example for ease of use. By pushing down on a foot treadle, the weaver opens the shed, leaving hands free to use the shuttle efficiently. Floor looms are usually wider and deeper than table looms and, in general, the deeper the loom, the more open the shed, which means that more tension can be exerted on the warp.

Loom Type I: A **jack floor loom** has one set of lamms. The "jacks" are devices either above the shafts to pull them down or below to push them up (illustration shows the latter). This type of loom is the most popular today, perhaps because it weaves a wide variety of weaving structures well. The shafts in the jack loom photographs move up and down in slots in the castle. With some jack looms, the shafts hang free in the center as we see with the counterbalance loom that follows.

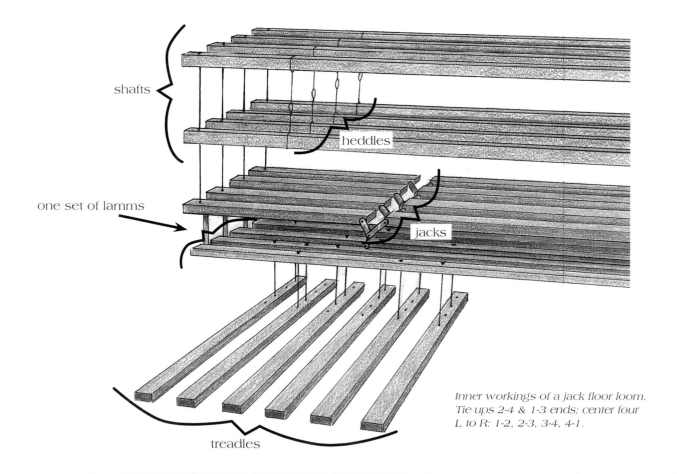

shafts

heddles

one set of lamms

jacks

treadles

Inner workings of a jack floor loom. Tie ups 2-4 & 1-3 ends; center four L to R: 1-2, 2-3, 3-4, 4-1.

This Schacht Baby Wolf X-frame portable jack loom is on wheels and folds up.

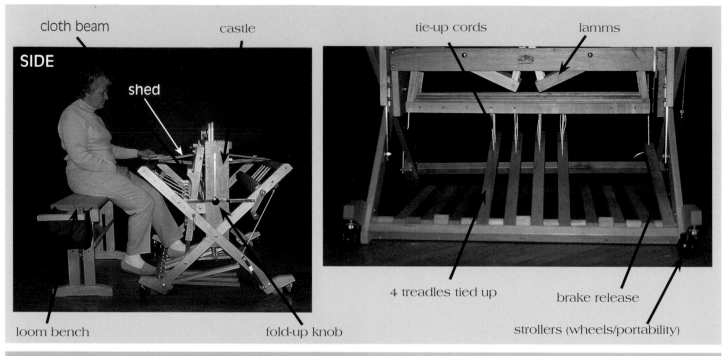

SIDE

cloth beam

castle

shed

loom bench

fold-up knob

tie-up cords

lamms

4 treadles tied up

brake release

strollers (wheels/portability)

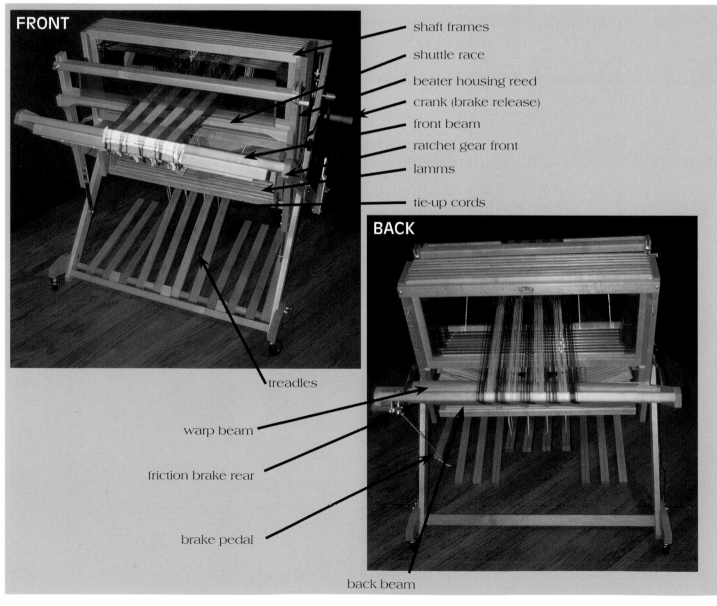

FRONT

shaft frames

shuttle race

beater housing reed

crank (brake release)

front beam

ratchet gear front

lamms

tie-up cords

treadles

warp beam

friction brake rear

brake pedal

BACK

back beam

Loom Type II: This **counterbalance floor loom** is shown with four shafts and usually weaves best with only four. Each set of two shafts works together as a pair. A cord connecting each pair either (1) runs over a pulley, (2) is attached to a short bar called a "horse," or (3) circles a roller. One treadle is attached to one shaft of a pair and, as it is pulled down, its corresponding shaft rises to balance it. This loom is excellent for any weave that requires lowering one shaft, which is the lower part of the shed, with its corresponding pair up, the upper part of the shed. Such a weave is called a **balanced weave** because the shaft pairs balance, half down and half up. This makes a nice, open shed.

For **unbalanced weaves**, however, it may be difficult to get a good shed on this type of loom. The treadle is tied so the loom lowers one shaft, sending the other up, but here we have both of the same pair trying to drop at the same time. To compensate for this, some use a **shed regulator**, which gets mixed reviews. Also, if there is no set of lamms, each treadle is tied directly to one shaft so the weaver must use two feet to activate more than one shaft at a time. Treadling on counterbalance looms is usually easy and light, but, if you are considering getting one, consider these limitations.

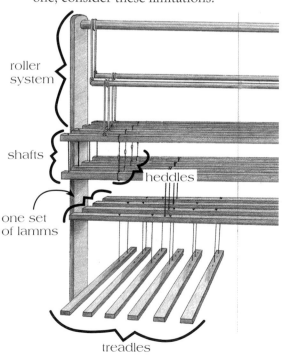

Inner workings of a counterbalance floor loom.

roller system

shafts

heddles

one set of lamms

treadles

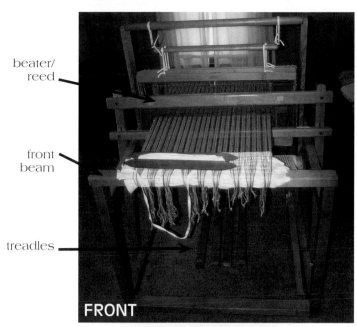

Hammett loom, typical, but no longer made, shows the roller method many prefer to minimize tilting of shafts on narrow warps.

beater/reed

front beam

treadles

FRONT

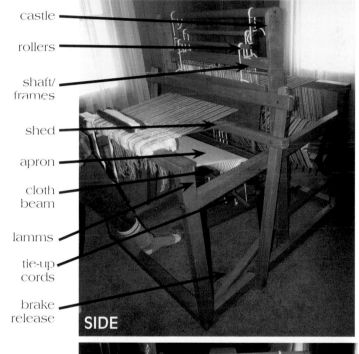

castle

rollers

shaft/frames

shed

apron

cloth beam

lamms

tie-up cords

brake release

SIDE

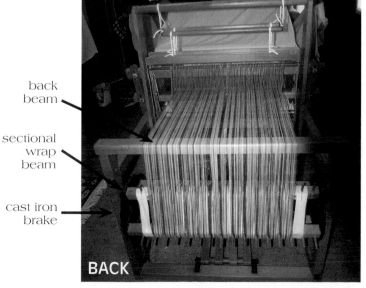

back beam

sectional wrap beam

cast iron brake

BACK

Loom Type III: A **countermarch floor loom** has two sets of lamms, one set positioned over the other. Each treadle is tied twice, once to each set of lamms. The top lamms are called "sinkers" (warp threads on those shafts drop); lower lamms are called "risers" (threads on those shafts rise).

The treadles on this loom activate the double set of lamms (one set rises and the other set sinks) that activate the "jacks" above that, in turn, activate the shafts. The norm for this loom is to tie up both risers and sinkers. It produces a wide shed with the least stress on warp threads since each shed opens only halfway under equal tension.

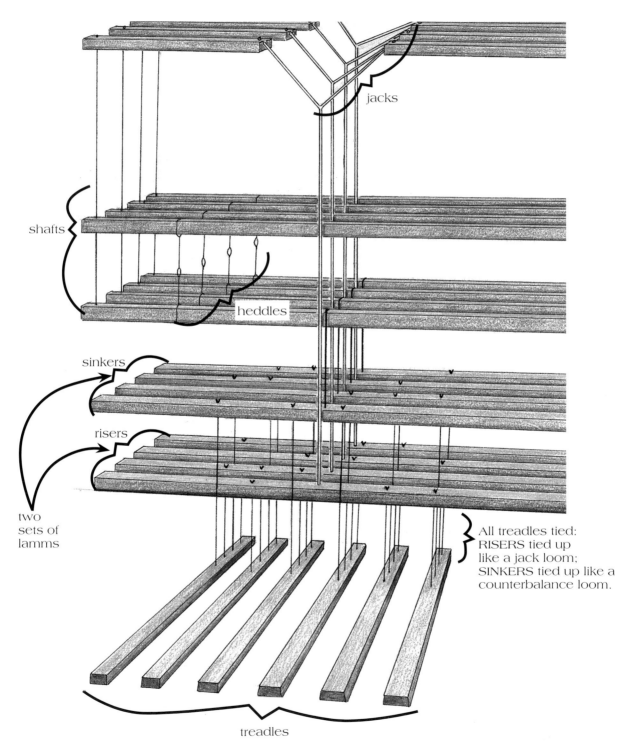

jacks

shafts

heddles

sinkers

risers

two sets of lamms

All treadles tied: RISERS tied up like a jack loom; SINKERS tied up like a counterbalance loom.

treadles

The inner workings of a countermarch floor loom.

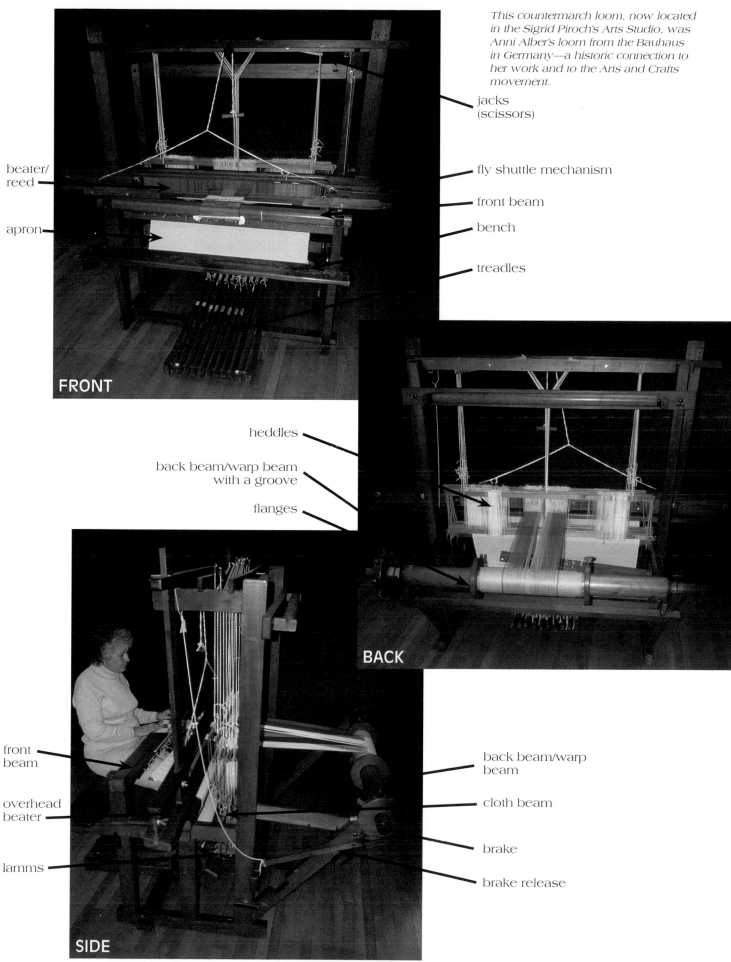

This countermarch loom, now located in the Sigrid Piroch's Arts Studio, was Anni Alber's loom from the Bauhaus in Germany—a historic connection to her work and to the Arts and Crafts movement.

jacks
(scissors)

fly shuttle mechanism

front beam

bench

treadles

beater/
reed

apron

FRONT

heddles

back beam/warp beam
with a groove

flanges

BACK

front
beam

overhead
beater

lamms

back beam/warp
beam

cloth beam

brake

brake release

SIDE

Photo courtesy of the Shelburne Museum, Shelburne, Vermont.

A jacquard mechanism mounted on a handloom with fly shuttle. This jacquard loom stands 9 feet high, 10 feet wide, and 10 feet long.

The number of treadles on a loom is usually the number of shafts plus two, so a 4-shaft loom has six treadles and an 8-shaft loom has ten. To find the number of shedding possibilities on any loom, use the formula 2 to the nth power minus <u>2</u> (sometimes written as 2n-2), where n is the number of shafts. The -2 is included because there is no shed with all shafts up or all shafts down. A 4-shaft loom has 14; an 8-shaft has 254; 12 has 4,094; 16 gets us to 65,534; 24 is over 16 million; and 32 is over four billion.

Computer-Assisted Handloom: In the 1970s, handweavers were among the first to apply computer technology in the arts. The jacquard head for the handloom became popular in the early 1800s using punched cards to activate any combination of threads for unlimited sheddings, so the weaver could create essentially any textile design. Jacquard technology is the forerunner of the automated loom that revolutionized the textile industry, and a precursor of the modern computer.

Today, many handweavers, including hobby weavers, design with software and may even weave on a shaft loom interfaced with a computer. The computer keeps track of the treadling no matter how long or complex. On an 8-shaft loom without a computer interface, there are usually ten treadles. But a computer-assisted loom has 254 possible treadle combinations. With a standard loom, after the first ten treadles are in use, the weaver must untie and retie treadles under the loom to weave other combinations. The result is that most weavers use only those original ten. A loom with more shafts has more treadles, but, especially with certain weaves, it may become difficult to keep track of the order for weaving them all. On an 8-shaft handloom with computer-assist and software, all 254 treadles are accessible *at all times, for each pick.* So every possible combination of shedding is always available. Plus, the computer also keeps track of the order in which they are used. Such a loom has only one, or, in some cases, two treadles that open the shed and advance to the next shed. A loom with a computer-assist is a popular option for handicapped weavers, those who wish to weave with more combinations and/or longer sequences, and even sometimes beginner weavers. Also popular are looms that have the option to upgrade to a computer-assist later.

A computer does repetitive tasks well, but it does not design for you, warp the loom for you, or weave for you. Not all weavers use a computer to design and not all who use a computer to design use one to weave.

For the first time in textile history, the handweaver need not produce textiles for the home or long runs of fabrics to sell, but can experiment and design at will. We are indeed on the "cutting edge" of new developments in this new century. With the evolution of new technical options and specialized threads on the one hand, and our rich textile history on the other, remarkable designs are possible.

Which Loom Should You Buy?

Buying a loom is a very personal decision. Among the factors that help you decide is what you want to weave. If you are a new weaver, you may not be sure yet. Don't worry; a good loom is a good investment and, should you want different equipment later, that loom will be just what another weaver is seeking. Keep in mind that an 8-shaft loom resells much faster than a 4-shaft loom. Even if you plan to weave with only four shafts, the extra shafts will come in handy for a variety of purposes that include using them for selvedges and spreading the warp out onto more shafts, like if threads tend to stick together. Statistics show that weavers, more often than not, sell their first loom to buy the loom they later decide is more appropriate for their needs. Statistics also show that weavers usually sell a 4-shaft to buy an 8-shaft; and, more recently, the trend is toward even more shafts. If you can't afford an 8-shaft, some manufacturers make a "four now, four later" model that comes ready to weave with four shafts, but can

be upgraded to eight. This is the best of both worlds and these looms also resell well. Look carefully at as many looms as you can, comparing all features. Some looms, for example, come apart for easy access when you thread them. If you can, talk with weavers about what features are important to them.

If you are looking for a used loom, you need answers to many questions. What kind of loom do you want? If you find one, are all the parts there? Do rusty heddles or pitted reeds need to be replaced? Used looms and information about them can often be obtained through area guilds located through the Handweaver's Guild of America. Guild members' experiences can be invaluable to you, plus you gain the additional benefits of friendships with others who enjoy weaving.

For new looms, check ads in a current issue of *Handwoven* magazine or *Shuttle, Spindle and Dyepot* magazine, and request catalogs. But there is no better way to know if the equipment is right for you than to try it out for yourself. Attend a regional or national conference and talk with resellers and other weavers. Convergence, the largest such conference sponsored by HGA, is held biennially in the even years in the United States or Canada.

Building your own loom? Loom plans are available (see *Resources* on page 144). Most people think building a loom is cost-effective until they give it a try. It is not unusual for someone to tell me after the fact that they no longer think it was a good idea because they had to buy all the heddles and metal working parts, including the brake, at retail pricing.

It may also be hard to know how well a particular loom will weave from working plans or how comfortable you will be weaving on it. Being familiar with a variety of looms will help you decide.

Loom Maintenance

All looms need a "tune-up job" from time to time: bolts tightened, moving parts lubricated, shafts balanced, and stretched/worn/rusted parts cleaned and replaced if needed. Some of this is obvious from checking over your loom carefully and watching your

loom at work. Check the owner's manual if you have one. If your loom manufacturer is still in business, they can provide you with detailed information and replacement parts. To locate them, watch for ads in handweaving magazines and check for information online as well as in weaving lists and chat forums.

Definitions of Basic Loom Parts

The **castle** is the central upright part of the loom that supports the shafts and lamms.

The **back beam** is that part of the loom at the back over which the warp rides on its way to the warp beam.

The **warp beam** is that part of the loom at the back where the warp is rolled on and stored until it is advanced to weave.

The **front beam** (also called the breast beam) is that part of the loom at the front over which the woven cloth rides on its way to the cloth beam.

The **cloth beam** is that part of the loom at the front around which the woven cloth is rolled on the loom and stored until it is cut off.

The **brake** on a loom is attached to one side of the warp beam at the back to hold the warp under tension until it is advanced:

1. A **wheel with spokes** set in a hole is a primitive, but very efficient method;
2. A **ratchet brake** is a wood or metal gear with a saw tooth appearance; most looms also use a ratchet at the front of the loom to hand-adjust warp

tension (see table loom photos on page 24);
3. A **friction brake** of flat or round wire encircles the warp beam on a metal track—this is an excellent type of brake, as the warp can be moved and held at any position along that continuum;
4. Any combination thereof.

Most looms have a **brake release**, often a stick with a cord attached to the brake at the back of the loom that can be activated by the weaver from the front to release the warp. A loom that permits ease in releasing the brake and moving the warp forward without getting up is preferable, since the warp should be moved often throughout weaving. Otherwise the edges of the warp may weave unevenly and edge threads show extra wear.

Ratchets, metal or wooden gears, are usually used at the front of a loom; attached around the cloth beam, they provide a means to adjust and fine-tension the warp from the front. Gears, located on the warp beam, may also be used to adjust tension at the back of the loom.

The brake (wheel with spokes) on Anni Albers's countermarch loom.

Friction brake on the Schacht Baby Wolf loom.

Definitions of Optional Loom Parts

A **shuttle race** is a narrow shelf at the base of the reed along the beater that supports the shuttle as it rides across the shed (see Schacht Baby Wolf loom on page 26). Not all looms have a shuttle race.

Flanges are seen on some looms or can be added if desired. Usually made of wood, they circle the warp beam, snugged up on either side of the warp to keep edge threads from slipping. The rod, on which the warp at the back of the loom is tied, is secured in a recess in the warp beam (see countermarch loom on page 29).

A **loom apron** is a length of fabric at weaving width attached to the cloth beam at one end; at the other end of this fabric a rod or stick is attached. Warp ends are tied onto this rod, or a rod attached to this rod, at the front of the loom.

A **second warp beam** can be mounted at the back of the loom to carry a second set of warp threads. Two types are shown below.

A **fly shuttle** is a device that propels one or more shuttles across a wide warp by pulling a cord at the center. This device is centuries old, developed because it is useful when the width of a fabric exceeds a weaver's reach.

Airlift is an option on some looms, especially looms with many, or heavy, shafts. Attached to a compressor, the loom uses air to lift the shafts. Cost for this can vary considerably from one manufacturer to another. It is helpful for some handicapped users.

Some looms have a built-in **bench** (such as the countermarch loom on page 29) but many benches are separate (such as the jack loom on page 26). They may be flat, slanted or sliding, adjustable or not, some with storage space. A bench is preferable to a chair or stool. The weaver is seated up over the warp; the weaver's bent elbows clear the front warp beam by several inches.

AVL's Studio Dobby loom (left); LeClerc's Nilart loom (right).

An extra warp beam is used when one set of warp threads interlaces less often than with another set, resulting in some threads loosening and resulting in uneven warp tension. An extra warp beam requires a second back beam over which that warp rides, plus a second brake and advancing mechanism. It is preferable to advance both warps from the front. A second back beam is not always needed since makeshift devices can be used, such as weighted rods slipped over looser threads.

A **sectional beam** is used for sectional warping (see the counterbalance loom on page 27 and the chapter on sectional warping).

The fly shuttle of a countermarch loom (top); a bank of 24 shafts on an AVL Studio Dobby loom, each four color-coded with label tape (bottom).

Color-coding the shafts may be useful, especially when there are many shafts. Some weavers dye or paint heddles different colors on different shafts to make it easier to locate any one during threading.

Glossary of Tools

A weaver should have the tool appropriate to do a specific job. But that does not mean you need lots of costly tools. Rather, obtain just the tools you need and add only what saves you time and consternation.

Shuttles come in a variety of shapes and sizes for different types of weaving. Yarn is wrapped around some shuttles, such as a stick shuttle. Another shuttle uses rotating **bobbins** filled with weft yarn that unwinds, without any tension, through a hole in the side (see page 79). An end-delivery shuttle uses stationary **pirns** to "deliver" the yarn through some sort of tensioner from an end-eye in the shuttle (see page 95).

How do you choose from such an array of

Right column: (1) huge rag mill shuttle *with room inside to pack rags; (2-6)* mill shuttles with metal tips *use pirns and some method of tensioning the yarn: brush tensioners, metal spring tensioners, multiple holes in the side, or multiple rods around which the yarn is twisted; (7-11) these* hand shuttles *use pirns with various built-in tensioners.*

Center column: (1-6) stick shuttles, *slow, but good for many types of weaving; (7)* pointed shuttle *is good for throwing through a shed, and also picking up threads for some types of weaving; (8)* roller shuttle, *shown upside down, speeds the shuttle along; (9)* shuttle with closed bottom *prevents drag from the bobbin on the lower shed; (10-11)* damask shuttles *are very shallow for narrow sheds—use a drinking straw or cardboard tube for the bobbin; (12-13)* double bobbin shuttles *weave with two bobbins at once.*

Left column: (1-5) boat shuttles *of various sizes use standard bobbins; up-pointed shuttle ends avoid catching threads if the bottom weaving shed is uneven; (6-7) for rags and heavy yarns,* rag shuttles; *(8)* rug shuttle, *and (9-10)* ski shuttles.

shuttles? Decide from the description which is best for your project; you will not need many. Rule out mill shuttles, sometimes available in antique shops—unless you have a fly shuttle—since metal tips can destroy warp edge threads. Standard boat shuttles with bobbins are probably the most popular. With these, you can weave with a variety of fine-to-medium threads. End-delivery shuttles with pirns are often preferred for fine-thread weaving, but can be used for a variety of purposes. The shuttles listed last are most often used with heavy yarns.

Warping Equipment: A **warping board** is most often used by a weaver to make a short or average-length warp to put on the loom. On it, you make the warp with the number of warp threads required for a design, each the same length. In this book, we use a 14-yard warping board which can create warps any length, from one to 14½ yards long; the length from a peg on the left to a peg on the right is one yard, with extra pegs across the top or bottom. Some warping boards come with fewer or more pegs for shorter or longer warps. Some have permanent pegs and some are removable, each with attendant advantages. Some only reach across a half-yard, requiring twice the number of passes to make a warp and double the amount of work. Some inkle looms double as warping boards.

You can make a warp of any length using a sectional system, within the limits of the warp beam and yarn package.

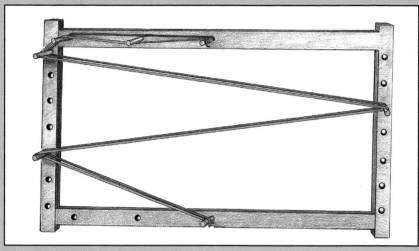

Warping board.

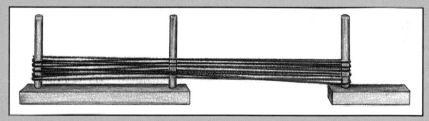

Don't have a warping board? You can make an excellent warp with warping pegs. *These are pegs that clamp on a table; they measure any given length for each thread and keep the weaver's cross.*

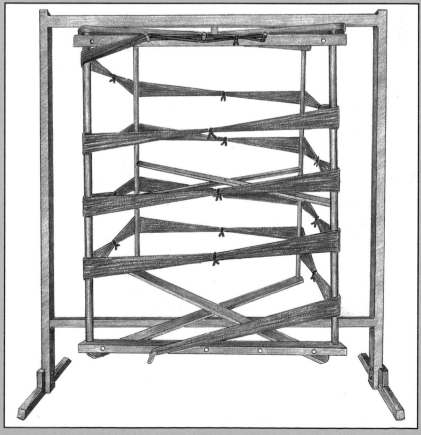

You can use a warping mill *for long warps.*

A **raddle** is used for the "back-to-front" method of warping a loom. It is a narrow length of wood, approximately the weaving width of the loom, with nails or pegs at half-inch or one-inch intervals. It is usually secured on the back beam, the front beam, or in the beater. It is used to contain and evenly space the warp so it rolls centered on the back beam. (Example: if we have a project sett at 24 ends per inch, then 24 warp threads are entered into each one-inch section of the raddle.) Some raddles have a top, which is placed on once the threads are in place; for others with no top, stretch and overlap rubber bands or slit clear tubing and slide over the teeth, to contain the threads. On an X-frame loom, the raddle can be mounted on the back beam.

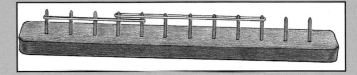

A raddle.

Winders help you wind, sometimes unwind, yarns.

A squirrel cage *(right)* has two circular barrels that rotate; these are attached to a post and can be adjusted up and down for each skein size. The skein circles from one barrel to the other, the cage holding it while it is skeined off.

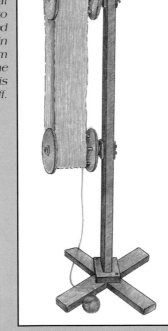

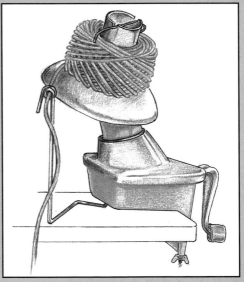

A ball winder *(left)* is handy because you have access to both yarn ends after the yarn is balled up.

A doubling stand *(left)* allows the natural twist in two or more yarns to wrap around each other to create a doubled yarn. Yarns are threaded one above the other through a center hole in each cone. A doubled yarn is used when you wish to vary the weft with a slight twist in the yarns, but not tightly, as with plied yarns.

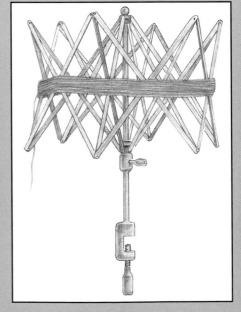

An umbrella swift *(left)* adjusts to hold a skein.

Some Neat Small Tools

System Texsolv®: These are Swedish products made of durable polyester cording, machine crocheted without knots. In addition to heddles, it is also made as a continuous chaincord of two parallel rows, forming a ladder of half-inch repeating holes that may be secured by nylon pegs or couplers. Because this product never stretches (it remains the same length even after considerable wear), its design minimizing friction. This cording is popular as heddles and for tying up loom parts temporarily and permanently.

In the photo at right, Texsolv cording is used to surround a piece of board secured with a straight peg (left); in the example (center), Texsolv goes through a hole and is secured with an anchor peg. A **sley** or **reed hook** (upper right) is a small hand tool used to pull warp ends through the reed. A **threading** or **warp hook** (center bottom) is an optional hand tool used to thread a warp end through a heddle. (Some weavers prefer to thread heddles with their fingers, some double over the end first.) Some tools have a sley hook at one end and a threading hook at the other. Wind yarns around an **inch gauge** (right) to determine **wraps-per-inch** (wpi). One-inch gauge measures one inch and two inches, the other one-inch and one-half inch. To cut threads, very sharp standard **scissors** are needed, especially to get a clean cut with silk; stork scissors are especially good with very fine threads (upper left). **Wax clips** (center right) are excellent to attach directions to a loom; quick to mount and remove, they leave behind only wax, which is good for wood. The blue **letter opener** is a great yarn cutter (lower left) and is available at office supply stores.

The **fringe twister** (bottom photo) makes twisting fringe a cinch, such as on these three handwoven color-and-weave effect silk scarves made by the author.

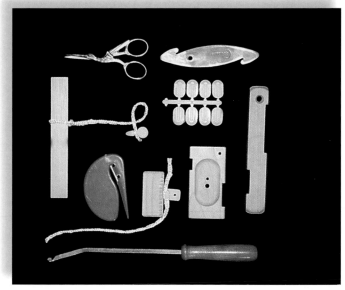

Clockwise from top: Scissors, sley or reed hook, wax clips, inch gauge, yarn gauge, threading or warp hook, Texsolv secured with an anchor peg, letter opener, Texsolv cording surrounding a piece of board.

Fringe twister.

Definitions of Weaving Terms

Each fabric varies according to the yarns used—fiber type, spinning method, color—as well as weaving method, sett, structure, and finishing. Understanding these terms will help you learn about weaving and how it is accomplished.

Paper weaving is a means of interlacing thin paper strips rather than yarns. This is a useful method to visualize how various types of weavings form different structures (see page 41).

Weaving structure is how threads interlace. Many woven structures have specific names to differentiate one type of interlacement from another.

The **weaver's cross** is essential to keeping warp ends in order as the warp is made—threads go *over* a peg in one direction and return *under* after traveling the length of the warp around other pegs. A second optional cross can be made in the warp.

Pattern weft is the weft used to create a pattern over a ground (background). **Ground weft** is the weft used to create the ground of a weaving when there is also a pattern.

A **one-shuttle weave** requires only one shuttle to weave. A **two-shuttle weave** requires two shuttles to weave ... and so on. Weaving progresses faster with one shuttle than with two.

Balance is the relationship between the numbers of warp ends to weft picks. If there are exactly the same type and number of warp ends per inch (epi) as weft picks per inch (ppi) in a textile, it is said to be a 50/50 weave, perfectly balanced.

If the weft covers the entire warp so only the weft is seen, the textile is said to be 100 percent **weft-faced**. If the warp covers the entire weft so only the warp is seen, it is said to be 100 percent **warp-faced**.

Other percentages, based on the number of warps in relation to the number of wefts, can also be used as **balance variations**. One way to change the balance is to change the sett. The closer the warp threads, the more warp-faced it becomes; that is, the more the warp shows in relation to the weft. The wider the sett, the more weft-faced it becomes; that is, the more the weft shows in relation to the warp.

Beat: To "beat" is to bring up the weft to the fell line of the cloth with the beater. However, the term "beat" can be a misnomer, as it can mean the weft is beaten hard as with most rug weaving, *or* the weft can be lightly beaten as with a soft wool, say for a throw, *or* it can be merely "placed" as with some very delicate fabrics.

Weavings Range from Delicate to Heavy-Duty

Ulrike Beck's "Serenity" transparency with slats, 36" wide x 51" long.

Photo by Dieter Beck.

Peter Collingwood's "Peace Rug SS-74" is a shaft-switched rug of wool on linen.

Weaving Structure and Sett

Pillow in miniature overshot with the original pattern developed from the words "Magic of Handweaving" into a draft.

A sampler of "The Magic of Handweaving" pattern in a three pattern-tabby color combination.

H ow threads interlace with one another to make cloth is called **structure**. There are many different woven interlacements, each a different structure. We use specific names to differentiate between them. This chapter shows some common structures with illustrations to show how they interlace, and later shows you how to weave the structures yourself. In the illustrations on the following pages, the gray vertical threads are warp; blue horizontal threads are weft.

Structure Definitions

In **plain weave**, every weft thread passes alternately over one warp thread and under one warp thread at the same time that every warp thread passes alternately under one weft thread and over one weft thread. On the next row, the sequence for both warp and weft is the opposite: under one, over one. This is the most basic of all weaves and the strongest, since no thread ever passes over more than one thread at a time in either direction.

In **twill weave**, every weft thread passes over two (or more) warp threads and under one (or more) warp threads, or vice-versa; on the next pick, the weft thread repeats the same sequence—one warp thread to the right (right-hand twill) or to the left (left-hand twill). Twills vary considerably in their complexity, but are usually easy to spot because threads appear as a diagonal in the cloth, sometimes reversing.

Plain weave.

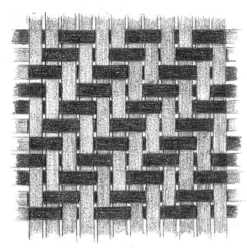

2/2 twill weave.

A **heading** is plain weave woven at the beginning and/or ending of a weaving, usually only for an inch or so. **Tabby** is another name for plain weave, usually used when this background thread is woven alternately with a pattern thread.

In **basket weave**, every pair of weft threads passes over and then under a pair of warp threads at the same time every pair of warp threads passes over and under a pair of weft threads. On the next row, both pairs of threads weave opposite.

In **supplementary weft weave,** a pattern weft is woven, usually alternately, with a background weft. If the pattern weft is removed, the cloth remains intact. In the illustration below, the darker threads are the pattern threads.

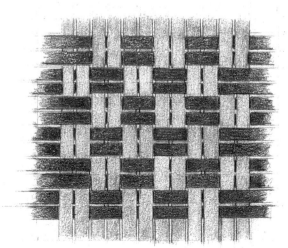

Basket weave.

Supplementary weft weave.

At left: plain weave (top left); 2/2 twill (top right); basket weave (bottom), turned "on point."

At right: 2/2 twill (left); basket weave (center); plain weave (right).

Paper Weaving

Before weaving structures with threads on a loom, you may wish to try paper weaving. Cut 1/4" to 1/2" strips of paper in dark and light, then in a variety of shades. Interlace as shown for these three structures.

Sett is the number of warp ends per inch (epi) in the reed. One way to estimate sett (epi) is by wrapping a yarn, representing warp, around a ruler. For accuracy, wrap for two inches with the yarn under light tension, threads just touching, but never overlapping; divide by two; this number is **wraps per inch** (WPI). Use WPI for a balanced plain weave sett, the norm from which all other weave setts are derived.

Estimate sett by wrapping yarn around a ruler.

1. In general, a **50/50 plain weave** (the same number of threads per inch in both directions) will be half the WPI number. If you get 20 WPI with a yarn, this weave structure will weave at 10 epi. Thus the many weaves that are a variation of plain weave will also use this sett, such as lace weaves and "Ms-and-Os."

2. **Twills** sett closer than plain weave, so using the plain weave WPI as our norm for this yarn, we can project that it will sett at 12-15 epi; a range is given to take into consideration yarn characteristics, width on the loom, and how compact you wish to weave your twill.

3. **Supplementary weft weaves** require a little wider sett than plain weave because, in addition to the plain weave ground, it must also accommodate the pattern weft; try 8 epi for this example.

4. **Weft-faced weaves** require the weft to cover the warp; half the WPI for 10 epi.

5. **Warp-faced weaves** require the warp to cover the weft; double 20 = 40, but is often higher.

With any yarn, as the ratio of the warp to the weft changes (sett), the look and feel of a fabric also changes. Since sett affects fabric qualities (thickness, weight, drape, etc.), the fabric purpose also changes. For example, a warp-faced textile makes a good rug, but not a good dress.

WPI is 24 for 3/2 cotton, so for 50/50 plain weave, the sett is 12 epi. Experience will also help you estimate sett. Sampling on the loom is essential to make a final determination. Some factors that influence sett include how much a yarn stretches/compresses, width on the loom, and beat.

To see how colors look next to each other before sampling, wrap yarns around cardboard using different colors, sequences, designs, and proportions; that is, different numbers of threads per color.

TIP

Sample on the loom with various color or size combinations for weft. For warp, cut out any warp thread and attach a new one, weighted, letting it hang over the back beam. It works well, for example, to add a heavy accent thread. Often you do not need to cut the thread already on the loom; just pull the new yarn through the heddle and over it. Though both weave together, the new thread stays on top. When done, cut and pull out the original from your sample. Or put various colors/sizes on the loom at the beginning and end of the warp, rolled on, but not threaded, then pull any one across and through a heddle to weave in for a few inches.

Maple Leaf Silks

Mary Bentley of Bowen Island, British Columbia, Canada, is celebrated for her use of spontaneous color in multi-shaft weaving, having spent 12 years focusing on this technique. Here are two polychrome Summer-and-Winter silk weavings.

"Shawl," 8-shaft with inlay and wools.

"Fuchsia Fantasy," 16-shaft with inlay and pickup.

Sett Chart: Use the Sett Chart on the following page to establish how many warp ends to put in each dent of a particular reed size for a particular sett. Dents per inch, from 5 to 20, are listed across the top; down the right side are listed various sleys for any given reed—that is, how many threads to put in each reed dent; columns indicate the result. You can begin with the reed you have and follow a column until you come to the ends per inch you are seeking.

Or, let's say you wish to sett a fabric at 12 ends per inch, as for the first sample in the sett project that follows. If you have a 12-reed, use one per dent; if you have a 6-reed, use two per dent; if you have an 8-reed, sley one in a dent and then two in a dent, repeat across; if you have an 18-reed, sley one in a dent, then one in a dent, then none in a dent and repeat across.

Sett Chart

Sett Chart: Ends per inch
Reed Size: Dents per inch →

5 DPI	6 DPI	8 DPI	10 DPI	12 DPI	15 DPI	18 DPI	20 DPI	Sley the Reed ↓
1¼ EPI	1½ EPI	2 EPI	2½ EPI	3 EPI	3¾ EPI	4½ EPI	5 EPI	1/0/0/0 & repeat
1⅔	2	2⅔	3⅓	4	5	6	6⅔	1/0/0
2½	3	4	5	6	7½	9	10	1/0
3⅓	4	5⅓	6⅔	8	10	12	13⅓	1/1/0
3¾	4½	6	7½	9	11¼	13½	15	1/1/1/0
5	6	8	10	12	15	18	20	1
6¼	7½	10	12½	15	18¾	22½	25	1/1/1/2
6⅔	8	10⅔	13⅓	16	20	24	26⅔	1/1/2
7½	9	12	15	18	22½	27	30	1/2
8⅓	10	13⅓	16⅔	20	25	30	33⅓	1/2/2
8¾	10½	14	17½	21	26¼	31½	35	1/2/2/2
10	12	16	20	24	30	36	40	2
11¼	13½	18	22½	27	33¾	40½	45	2/2/2/3
11⅔	14	18⅔	23⅓	28	35	42	46⅔	2/2/3
12½	15	20	25	30	37½	45	50	2/3
13⅓	16	21⅓	26⅔	32	40	48	53⅓	2/3/3
13¾	16½	22	27½	33	41¼	49½	55	2/3/3/3
15	18	24	30	36	45	54	60	3
16¼	19½	26	32½	39	48¾	58½	65	3/3/3/4
16⅔	20	26⅔	33⅓	40	50	60	66⅔	3/3/4
17½	21	28	35	42	52½	63	70	3/4
18⅓	22	29⅓	36⅔	44	55	66	73⅓	3/4/4
18¾	22½	30	37½	45	56¼	67½	75	3/4/4/4
20	24	32	40	48	60	72	80	4
21¼	25½	34	42½	51	63¾	76½	85	4/4/4/5
22½	27	36	45	54	67½	81	90	4/5
21⅓	26	34⅔	43⅓	52	65	78	86⅔	4/4/5
23⅓	28	37⅓	46⅔	56	70	84	93⅓	4/5/5
23¾	28½	38	47½	57	71¼	85½	95	4/5/5/5
25	30	40	50	60	75	90	100	5

Sett Project

To illustrate how sett works in "real time," I designed a striped warp to weave at various setts. This warp has 12 threads of each color—green, white, red, white, green, white, red, white, green—a total of 108 threads. I made a warp 6 yards long, for six samples with fringe and hemstitching, of 3/2 cotton (1,260 yd./lb.) taking into account take-up, loom waste, finishing, and cutting off between most samples to re-sley as needed. I threaded this in straight twill (1, 2, 3, 4, and repeat).

All samples were woven with the same weft threads as warp, same colors, same sequence, and same number of threads:

1. Balanced plain weave at 12 epi—9" wide;
2. Basket weave at 15 epi—just over 7";
3. 2/2 twill at 15 epi—same as last;
4. Warp-faced at 66 to 84 epi—about 1⅔" to 1¼";
5. Weft-faced at 6 epi—18" and
6. Supplementary weft weave at 10 epi—almost 11".

Plain weave sample, which is the sett norm.

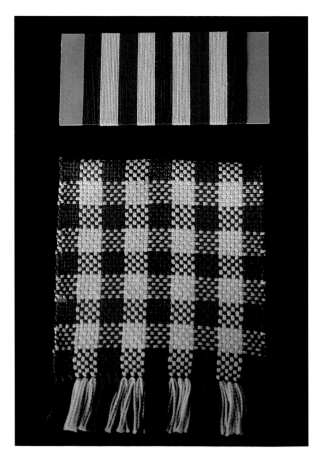

Basket weave sample with color wrapping. The sett for 50/50 basket weave is closer than 50/50 plain weave because in basket weave, each thread interlaces with every other thread.

2/2 twill sample. In 2/2 twill, one weft thread is over two and under two, moving diagonally. This twill skips over and under two threads, as does basket weave, so both have the same sett of 15.

Warp-faced and **weft-faced** plain weave fabrics are stiffer than plain weave or twill and are more durable. The structure for these warp and weft-faced textiles is identical to plain weave.

To cover weft entirely in a warp-faced textile, you must sett the warp close. Here, it is so close that I didn't need to use a reed at all, just like with band weaving. Weft doesn't show except a little at the edges, so the same color weft is used as warp. Since only the striped warp shows, the colors weave vertical stripes.

Supplementary weft weaving begins with a one-inch **heading**, 1-3 and 2-4. Then a pick of pattern weft is thrown on 1-2, a pick of plain weave (tabby) on 1-3, again pattern 1-2, then the other tabby 2-4. Pattern 1-2 is repeated as desired and forms Block A until the next twill combination 2-3 is used for Block B, also with alternating tabbies; then 3-4 for Block C and finally 4-1 for Block D. This is the same threading as all previous samples, but woven with a **standard tie-up:** treadle 1 tied to shafts 1-2, treadle 2 to 2-3, treadle 3 to 3-4 and treadle 4 to 1-4; tabby is 1-3 tied to treadle 5 and 2-4 to treadle 6.

Although threaded and woven with the same yarns and colors, these fabrics are very different. We have pushed the sett from 6 epi to 86 epi and the width on the loom from 18" to 1¼". This project shows the importance of sett in achieving the result you want in a weaving project—how your fabric looks, how it feels, and what is appropriate for its use.

Warp-faced plain weave band at 66 epi (left) using a ruler to maintain exact bandwidth; warp-faced plain weave band with even closer spacing—up to 84 epi (right).

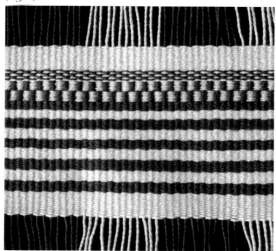

This weft-faced color-and-weave effect sample is sett wide at 6 epi. Begin at the bottom: as it packs down over the warp, only the weft is seen, so repeating the same color weaves a horizontal stripe. Next, the weft-faced textile is woven pick-and-pick—one pick of one color yarn (one throw of the shuttle) alternates with one pick of another color. Red and white alternate, then white with green, for vertical stripes. Finally all three colors rotate—green, red, white—to create a pattern.

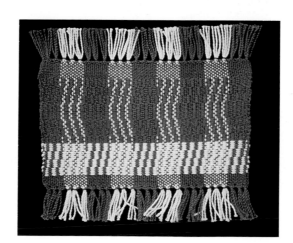

The supplementary weft weave sample is sett a little wider than plain weave at 10 epi to allow room for the pattern to skip in and out. Tabby weft is the same size as warp; pattern weft is usually heavier than warp so it is doubled here. In this sample, I used green tabby with the four twill pattern blocks that form on four shafts—white, red, and then green.

Drafting and Drawdowns

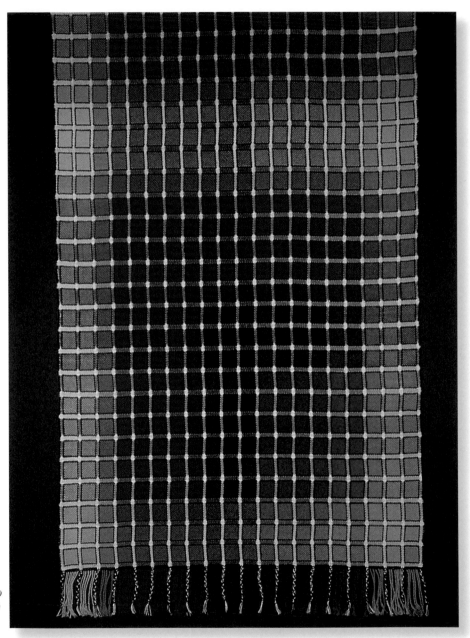

"Window Panes" by Blanche Hall uses 20 colors of cotton from Lunatic Fringe.

For centuries, weavers have found ways to document weaving. Such a notation method is called *drafting*. Thankfully, drafting today has become standardized. In order to thread a loom and weave fabric, you must be able to read a weaving draft. Let's take a closer look at what makes up a draft, and apply it to four basic weaves: plain weave, basket weave, 2/2 twill, and supplementary weft.

A **weaving draft** is a notation method on graph paper showing how a loom is threaded, tied up, and treadled for a particular cloth. A draft has four parts:

1. The **threading area** shows each warp thread in order and on which shaft;
2. The **tie-up area** shows which shafts, one or more, are connected to each treadle;

3. The **treadling area** shows which treadle to use in what order; and
4. The **drawdown area** shows the cloth structure—the position of every warp and weft thread in relation to every other.

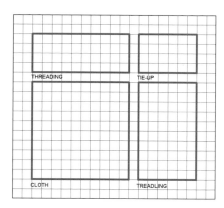

The four weaving draft quadrants.

Each type of draft provides a different visualization of the textile. The *drawdown* area of a draft can be represented in these basic ways:

1. A **structural drawdown** here represents the weft threads as dark and the warp threads as blank;
2. A **color-and-weave-effect drawdown** shows the color placement of the warp and weft in relation to the structure;
3. An **interlacement drawdown** shows the structure as horizontal weft lines and vertical warp lines;
4. A **color-and-weave interlacement drawdown** shows the horizontal and vertical lines as threads interlaced in color; and/or
5. A **sidewinder drawdown** shows the threads, warp and/or weft, looking at the cloth from the side or edge.

Use a structural draft as your basic means of drafting.

The tie-up of the three basic types of looms affects how we view and work with each draft. When the weaver pushes down on a treadle, one or more shafts that carry warp threads are activated and this creates a *shed*, an opening for the shuttle to pass through.

1. A jack loom lifts one or more shafts while the other shafts remain at rest.
2. A counterbalance loom drops one or more shafts while the corresponding shaft of that pair rises; if any one of a pair is not activated, the pair remains at rest.
3. A countermarch loom lifts one or more shafts and drops all others.

In the *tie-up area* of a draft, we indicate all working shafts for that loom by these symbols:
1. **O** is used for a jack loom tie since each active treadle lifts the working shaft(s) like a balloon.
2. **X** is used for a counterbalance loom tie since each active treadle drops the working shaft(s) like an anchor.
3. Both an **O** and an **X** are used as ties for a countermarch loom since each treadle is tied up to both sets of the lamms, the *risers* and *sinkers*. (See the labeled illustrations of the three loom types on pages 25, 27, and 28).

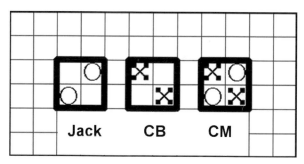

Tie-ups for plain weave on two shafts for jack, counterbalance, and countermarch looms.

The following exercises use a jack loom. We will draft *weft drawdowns*, in which the weft thread is on the top in the draft, or the face of the cloth. We will use numbers in the threading, tie-up, and treadling areas of the draft. (Note: A solid block in the threading, tie-up, or treadling areas sometimes represents a profile draft, a different type of drafting explained later in this chapter.)

On most floor looms, you can tie up more than one shaft to each treadle. Some looms have only a direct tie-up—each treadle tied to only one shaft. To activate more than one shaft for any shed, you must use two feet. Most table looms have a lever that lifts just one shaft at a time and you can easily activate more than one at the same time.

Structural Draft

In this draft, the drawdown shows the warp and weft threads on the face of the fabric as if looking down on it. Squares can be filled in various ways to represent this as shown in the illustration below. These symbols are used to indicate each warp and weft in drawdowns throughout this book. A square that represents a weft is either a dot or a solid or horizontal line pair. A square that represents a warp is either left blank or shown as a vertical pair of lines.

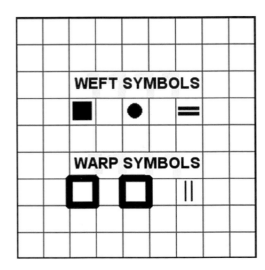

Warp and weft draft symbols.

Let's begin with a plain weave draft on two shafts: a structural draft with a jack tie-up. In plain weave, a thread alternates above and below the face of the cloth in each direction. To represent the wefts, one type of draft shows dots and the other type shows solids. Both are used, so which is best?

The Dot Method

By hand, I always prefer to draft using a dot, then make any *adjacent* dots into solids. (When learning, draft by hand using the dot method.) When a thread sits alone on top, it looks like a dot on the surface of the cloth. When two or more threads sit side-by-side, there is a skip in the cloth that looks more like a solid. In a plain weave draft, no thread ever skips over more than one thread, but in all other weaves, two or more dots will come together at some place and can be filled in solid. (Computer drafting generally uses solids or directional threads, not dots.)

The *mini-box* outlined in the upper right of the drawdown area of any draft represents one repeat of the threading and treadling. A **repeat** is the smallest number of ends and picks that form one complete pattern. Plain weave has the smallest repeat. No matter the warping method, the draft is read and threaded the same.

The top left threading quadrant from right to left reads 1, 2 across. When you thread the loom, proceed right to left, putting one thread in the first heddle on the first shaft, then the next thread in the first heddle on the second shaft; the third thread goes in the next heddle on the first shaft; the fourth thread goes in the next heddle on the second shaft, and so on. (If you are left-handed, you may find it easier to read and thread from the left.) The top right tie-up quadrant indicates the first shaft is tied to the first treadle and the second shaft is tied to the second treadle. The right treadling quadrant gives the sequence of treadling: 1, 2, and repeat. The center drawdown area shows the structure of the cloth that results.

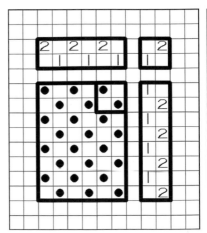

The dot method.

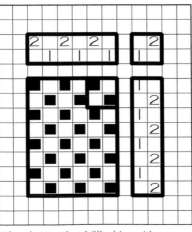

The dot method filled in with solids, as in some computer drafts.

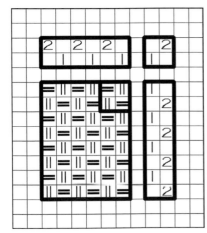

An interlacement draft.

Interlacement Draft

In an this draft, the drawdown shows the direction of each warp and weft thread as seen on the face of the cloth. When handweavers draft only by hand, they may be reluctant to do time-consuming interlacement drafting, though mills use them extensively. Today most weaving software drafting programs generate these quickly, making them valuable tools frequently used by handweavers at all levels once they can draft by hand.

Color-and-Weave Effect Draft

This draft shows three warp and weft colors as they appear on the face. In this computer-generated draft, **color bars** above the threading area and to the right of the treadling area indicate the color of each warp and each weft thread. (Color bars may be located instead between the threading and drawdown area, or the treadling and drawdown areas.) In some drafting programs, the threading and treadling are colored.

Working by hand, you can log into these color bars other information you wish to remember, such as the type and the ply of yarn. This use of a bar for purposes other than color is common when working from a textile to develop an analysis draft (see Chapter 13.)

Color-and-Weave Interlacement Draft

In this draft, the drawdown shows the colors for that structure as thread interlacements. It is a combination of the last two drafting methods.

Sidewinder Draft

Another way to view thread interlacements in cloth is with a **sidewinder draft**. Think of viewing the drawdown from the edge or side of the cloth. If you give a mental tug to the red weft thread winding horizontally across the top, it becomes evident which green warp threads are on top and which are below in this pick of the fabric.

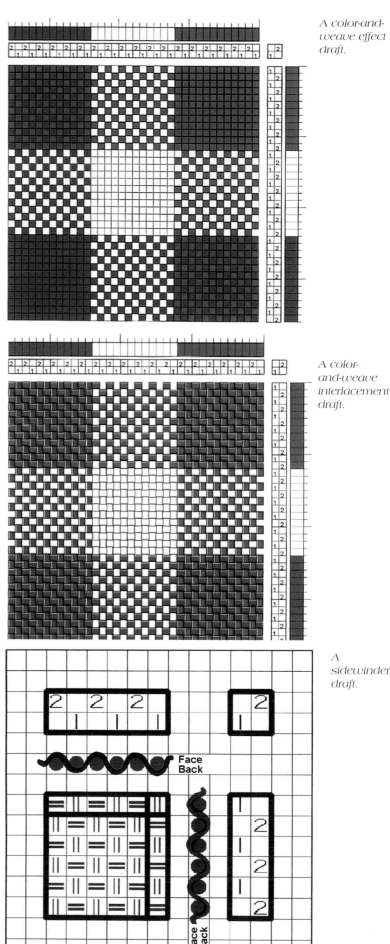

A color-and-weave effect draft.

A color-and-weave interlacement draft.

A sidewinder draft.

Each of the drafts in this chapter is a weft drawdown of a structural draft for a jack loom. The weft on top is represented as a dot or solid in the squares; blank squares represent warp. If this were reversed for a warp drawdown, the warp would be marked as a dot or solid and the blank squares would be weft. Both methods are correct, but use only one at a time.

In some cases, one type of drawdown provides better information than another, or you may use several drafts of the same fabric to better visualize it. For example, all-red warp and weft in a color-and-weave-effect drawdown will look red all over. A color-and-weave-effect interlacement drawdown lets you see the direction and intersection of each warp and weft.

Draw-Up Draft

So far, drafts fit the norm, but you can relocate quadrants while still maintaining the integrity of the draft. For example, you can place the threading at the bottom and the tie-up at the lower right with the treadling developed from the bottom up. This **draw-up draft** looks more like how a cloth actually weaves forward and up on a loom. Some weavers prefer this when working with a computer-interfaced loom, tracking the cloth as they weave it.

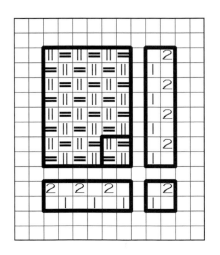

This draw-up draft looks more like how cloth actually weaves forward and up on a loom.

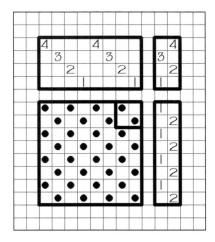 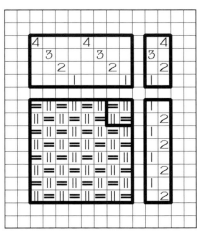

You can weave a plain weave sample on more shafts than two. These three drawdowns (two above and one below) use four shafts and are structurally identical to those on two shafts.

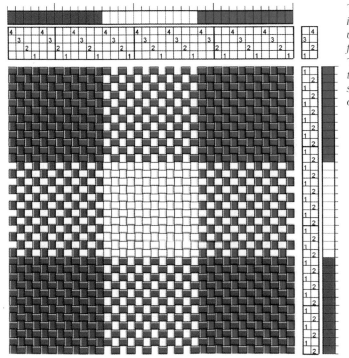

The color-and-weave interlacement draft shows plain weave as woven on four shafts for the sett project in Chapter 3. This allows weavers to weave the other three structures on the same warp: basket weave, twill, and supplementary weave.

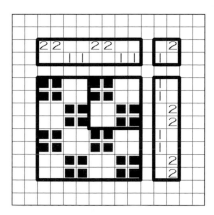

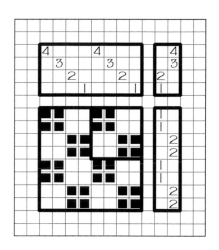

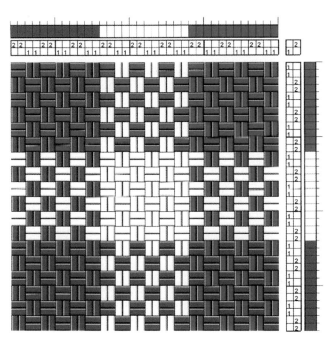

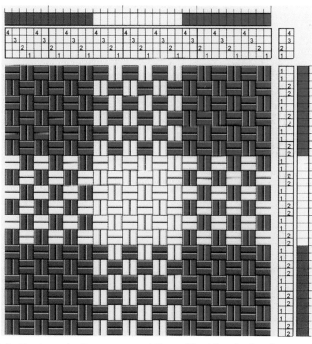

Basket weave *woven on two shafts (left) and on four shafts (right). On two shafts, you must thread just for the basket weave, while on four shafts you can thread straight twill one to four, making it possible to weave many other structures.*

WEAVERS AROUND THE WORLD

Before yarns can be put on a loom, each must be measured in length; this is called making a warp.

This weaver in Nebaj, Quiché, Guatemala is making a colorful warp.

2/2 twill requires four shafts because it needs four shed combinations for the full structure.

These two drafts differ in that one shows the plain weave woven with treadles 1 and 2; the other shows it as 1 and 6. Either is correct, but the latter draft is set up for **walking rhythm.** In walking rhythm, the weaver treadles left and right for plain weave as the shuttle is thrown right and left, just like swinging your arms while walking.

Often with pattern weaves, it is assumed the weaver knows to throw an alternate tabby between pattern weft rows, so the tabby is not shown in the draft. Two pattern blocks are shown: Block A = 1, 2 and Block B = 3, 4.

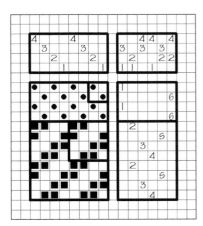

The mini-boxes in the drafts show the minimum repeat for plain weave and twill.

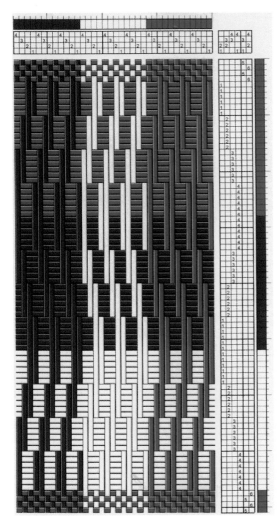

A quick reference draft of the four blocks of just the pattern wefts (above); two of the four pattern wefts and tabby weaving (below).

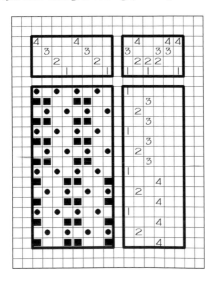

The color-and-weave interlacement draft is shown as woven in the sett chapter (left).

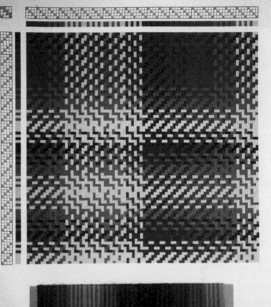

Computer-generated structural, interlacement, and color-and-weave effect drafts are shown, each with one possible threading and treadling for that yarn wrapping. Imagine how quickly you can try out alternatives and develop your own designs using this method.

Virtual designs with actual woven textiles include one by Norma Long, a student in my workshop at Forum '95 in Mittagong, Australia, who selected her favorites from a computer printout and wove them into this sampler (above).

Drafting with Computer Software

Drafting is an absorbing process. Some drawdowns, however, take a lot of time and graph paper to make by hand, especially color-and-weave effect interlacement drawdowns, which first require a structural drawdown so you know where to place each color. Drafting by hand helps you best learn and understand the process, but many weavers today use a computer drafting program because it works quickly and encourages exploration of structure, color work, and design.

Profile Drafting

There is one other type of draft called a *profile draft*. Although we do not use it in this book, you need to differentiate a profile draft from a thread-by-thread draft when you see one.

In a thread-by-thread draft, the type we have used until now, each square with a number represents one thread. In a *profile draft*, each square with a solid block represents a *unit* of threads. A profile draft is a shorthand method that shows overall design. Into a profile, you can plug in the threading, treadling, and tie-up for any weaving structure consisting of units that repeat regularly. Unit weaves include: "Summer and Winter," "Ms and Os," "Satin," "Lace" (Huck, Swedish, and Bronson), "Spot Weave," "Crackle," "Canvas Weave," "Doubleweave," "Lampas," "Beiderwand," and others. This type of draft is not used to thread directly on the loom, but instead depends on first substituting threading units for a particular weave.

Remember two things in profile drafting: (1) rather than numbers, solid blocks are used in the threading, tie-up, and treadling areas; (2) rather than numbers, capital letters indicate the blocks. Once a profile is converted to a regular draft, numbers are used once again. All profile drafts are shown as warp block drawdowns.

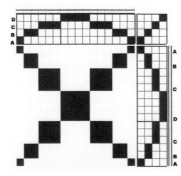

A profile draft, like a standard draft, is made up of the same four areas.

Threading Area: The threading area of this profile draft has four horizontal levels that represent four blocks, reading from the bottom up: Block A, Block B, Block C, and Block D. (More blocks in the design equal more levels.) Counting from the right, Block A is threaded once equalling one unit, Block B is threaded twice equalling two units, Block C is threaded three times equalling three units, Block D is threaded four times equalling four units, then it reverses. In this type of drafting, pattern blocks develop and are shown against a ground. The unit for the selected weave can be plugged into each threading block. Weaves threaded from profile drafts are often either contrasting in pattern, as with "Summer and Winter" pattern blocks, or in structure, as with "Bronson Lace" blocks, both on a plain weave ground.

Treadling Area: Figuring from the top down, Block A is the first vertical column on the left of the treadling area, treadled once; Block B, C, and D follow next, each adding in one more block, just as we did for the threading, then reversing. The unit for the selected weave can be plugged into each treadling block.

Tie-up Area: Again, each block in this area represents a unit that ties up the treadles. Each is unique to the weave. Each block in this tie-up weaves one block in the cloth, since each is tied up separately. In some weaves, like overshot, only one block can be woven at a time. In other weaves, such as double weave, more than one block can be woven at the same time.

Drawdown Area: This shows the overall block design that results.

Handspinner from Karjeeling in northern India spins yarn for carpet weaving at the Tibetan Refugee Self-Help Centre.

Photo by Dana McCown of Queensland, Australia.

WEAVERS AROUND THE WORLD

Much yarn is required for weaving, but first fibers must be prepared and spun (twisted) into yarn. In many parts of the world, spinning is still done by hand, even for rugs.

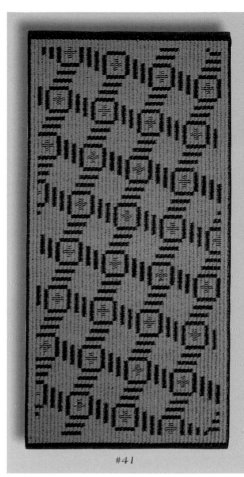

#41

#23

New Design Concepts

Jason Collingwood carries on his father's rug weaving traditions with new design concepts. These are two of his inspirational 40" x 80" (approximate) shaft-switched rugs of wool on linen.

"Summer and Winter" is a weave structure used to substitute from this profile draft into a thread-by-thread draft. Traditionally in this weave, shafts 1 and 2 carry the **tie-down threads**, warp threads that catch the weft pattern thread at regular intervals so it doesn't float too long, thus tying it down. Weft skips across 3 and under 1, tying down every fourth thread. The other shafts carry the *pattern* threads that make up the Block A, B, C and D designs. In "Summer and Winter," Block A is threaded 1-3-2-3, Block B is threaded 1-4-2-4, Block C is threaded 1-5-2-5, and Block D is threaded 1-6-2-6, each a four thread unit repeat. So a four block design in "Summer and Winter" requires a loom with six shafts. Now let's plug in "Summer and Winter," re-writing it as we would thread it on the loom and treadling it as birdseye, one of the traditional treadlings for this weave. A thread is added at the end to balance the pattern.

Two pillows with the same four-block profile draft/design, but woven as overshot (left) and diaper twill (right). Overshot uses only two threads for each profile block, while diaper twill uses four. So even though both pillows are woven at the same sett and with the same size threads, the pillow design on the right is twice as large in both directions.

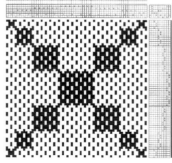

Draft of "Summer and Winter" weave.

Some structures need more shafts for each unit substitution than others. With profile drafting, you can design a pattern and then decide how you want to weave it. Some think it is much easier to design, draft, and thread from profiles. Practice with various drafts, then make up your own to become proficient.

5 Yarns, Threads and Fibers

"Anniversary Glitz Silk Jacket," 22-shaft, of turquoise inwoven with sequins in doubleweave. (Woven by Sigrid Piroch; modeled by Christen Piroch.)

Weavers use a wide variety of yarns and threads, but what is yarn? What are yarn size designations? And how can we use that information for weaving?

Yarn can be spun of whatever fiber you name. There are so many kinds of fibers and so many ways to spin yarn, that yarn types are almost unlimited. Yarns come in a vast array of singles (one strand twisted one direction) and plies (two or more twisted strands twisted again, usually the other direction)—boucles, loops, novelties, variegates, chenilles, high-tech industrials, and more. Handweavers mostly use yarns of natural fibers including flax, cotton, silk, wool, mohair, angora rabbit, alpaca, and llama; even dog hair and milkweed can be spun and woven. Hair fibers such as goat, yak, and camel work well for some purposes such as rug weaving. Some fibers are wondrously soft like camel down, cashmere, and qiviut (musk ox). Imported fibers include ramie, sisal, jute, kenaf, raffia, henequen, bamboo, hemp, banana and pineapple fibers (piña), reeds, and grasses. Sheep's wool in its many forms is one of the most popular, not only because it is easy to spin, but also because it takes dye well and weaves like a dream. Without chemical processing, virgin wool from selected breeds need not be

Different "put-ups" of yarns (cone, tube, skein, ball) with a stand to hold tubes and cones while working with them.

itchy, just one reason why spinners enjoy processing and spinning their own fibers. Spinners can also create most yarns affordably, including fancy designer yarns.

Some millspun natural yarns are mixes like cottolin—cotton mixed with short fibers of flax and silk-and-wool which, when dyed, take the dye differently to create heathery yarns. Cotton-covered sewing thread (high-quality long cotton fibers over a polyester core) is a good warp that may stretch, but rarely breaks. Tencel™ (lyocell) is a newer fiber made from reforested trees that looks and acts like a blend of lustrous silk and cotton; the surface micro-pills for a soft, silky, and sensuous fabric. Many beautiful new yarns are on the horizon, such as "soy silks" made from recycled products, considered environmentally friendly.

Be alert to characteristics of each fiber type and select a yarn size suitable for your purpose. For example, plan a rug using heavy linen rug yarn as warp, heavy wool rug yarn as weft, and choose a design suitable for a rug and a weaving structure that will wear well. For a soft, lacy shawl, you might select fine wool yarn for both warp and weft and a lacy pattern. Weaving magazines and books provide project ideas. Use these as guidelines rather than recipes.

It is important to know how each yarn is spun. Worsted wool is hardwearing and lustrous because long fibers are combed and spun straight, while woolens are soft and warm because shorter fibers are carded. Wet-spun line linen will produce a crisp, fine tablecloth, while dry-spun linen, usually heavier and fuzzier, makes great place mats. Some silk thread is very strong and lustrous, wonderful for garments, but not all silk threads are alike in quality or sheen.

Yarn Sizes

Weaving requires yards of yarns, so it is most practical to acquire it in larger packaging. Understanding what numbers mean for different yarn sizes can help you relate to relative sizes of all yarns in "real time."

Yarns come in standard sizes called "yarn counts." The many different yarn count systems can be quite confusing because they often differ by fiber type. The first yarn used for weaving in this book is 5/2 cotton. The 5 is the count or size of the yarn; the 2 tells us it is a 2-ply yarn. In the cotton count system, this yarn runs 2,100 yards per pound. The count of cotton is based on the spinning of one pound of cotton into 840 yards of No.1 yarn; other sizes are figured from this formula. A #5 yarn then is 840 multiplied by 5 equalling 4,200; because it is plied, divide by 2 for a final total of 2,100 yards per pound. (#2 cotton singles have twice the yardage of #1 cotton, 2 x 840 = 1,680 yards per pound. But there is no division for singles yarn.)

The McMorran Yarn Balance.

used. If you do not have information for a particular yarn, use the McMorran Yarn Balance to quickly calculate yards per pound. This small plastic box has a balance arm and metal pivot.

Place the arm in the small grooves on the box. On the edge of the arm, place a length of yarn and trim until it balances perfectly. If it is a long piece, set the balance on the edge of a table or fold it over on itself. To figure the number of inches, multiply 100 for the approximate yards per pound. If you place 5/2 yarn on a McMorran Yarn Balance it will be about 21" long; multiply it times 100 for 2,100 yards per pound. If yarn length is 8", then the yarn will be in the range of 800 yards per pound so, if you need 1,200 yards for a project, you will need a pound and a half of this yarn. Though this is also a good solution for mill ends and non-standard yarns, it is less reliable for handspuns since they can vary throughout. Remember, it's less important to have technical information than to be able to calculate yardage and estimate how much you need.

Linen count is based on the formula of 300 yards spun from one pound of raw flax. Jute, hemp, ramie, and grass linen are calculated on the linen count. Denier, the number of grams in 9,000 meters of yarn, is the universal system for measuring silk, rayon, and nylon. There are several count systems for wool, all standards established long ago. Formulas range from 560 yards worsted spun from one pound of raw wool, to 256 for woolen, to 300 for the cut system and 1,600 for the run system. But you seldom know which is

The Tex System figures yarn size for all types based on its linear density, or weight per unit length (the weight in grams of one kilometer or 1,000 meters). So if one kilometer of yarn weighs 100 grams, it is designated as 100. Unfortunately, although this system has been around for many years and could standardize all yarns, those available to weavers are still a mix. Yarn size is not straightforward, but you will become quickly tuned in to yarn size as you work with yarns. Collect samples from retailers. Sample and weave with quality yarns to achieve quality results.

What is the difference between a 5/2 and a 2/5 yarn? Placing the yarn size (5) first is typical in the United States and is used in this book; placing the number of plies (2) first is typically Canadian. Both are the same size yarn. The smaller number in a yarn designation is usually the number of plies.

Yarn Chart

Some standard yarn sizes follow as per manufacturer's guidelines with approximate yardages. Even standard sizes vary in characteristics, including length, from mill to mill. Some 20/2 cottons, for example, are softer or have less twist than others. Some cottons are mercerized and some are not. Those mercerized are more lustrous, stronger, and shrink less, but may also cost more. Wet-spun yarns are made of long fibers and are spun wet, smoother and stronger than dry-spun yarns. Some ramie and linen used to be spun wet and is now spun dry, changing the look and feel of the fibers and, consequently, how it looks in the weaving.

Yarn sizes	Fiber type	Yards per pound
3/2	Cotton	1260
5/2	Cotton	2100
8/2	Cotton	3360
8/4	Cotton (Carpet Warp)	1680
10/2	Cotton	4200
16/2	Cotton	6720
20/2	Cotton	8400
50/3	Cotton	14000
Cum Rya	Wool	570
6/2 and 7/2	Wool	1600-1640
12/2	Wool	3000 or 3360
16/2	Wool	4480
18/2 and 20/2	Wool (worsted system)	5040-5600
12/2	Silk	3000
20/2 or 30/2	Silk	7500
18/2	Silk and Wool	5040
16/2	Ramie	2400
20/3	Ramie	2000
22/2	Cottolin	1750
8/4 and 8/5	Linen	480-600
10/2	Linen (Dry Spun)	2100
14/2	Linen	2100
16/2	Linen	2400
20/2	Linen (Line)	3000
40/2	Linen (Line)	6000

Yarn characteristics include fiber, type, length, quality, preparation for and method of spinning, and dyes used. Even before spinning, silk varies by type, whether cultivated or wild (such as tussahs), by natural color, length, the part of the cocoon selected, and whether reeled or broken. Wool yarns may be worsted or woolen-spun, so it is important to know the characteristics of each.

WEAVERS AROUND THE WORLD

In many countries, yarn is still dyed by hand with natural dyes.

Natural dyes yield rich tones as with these yarns drying in the sun in Morocco, destined to be woven into prayer rugs.

Photo courtesy of Simplicity Pattern Co., Inc.

Finishing Fabrics

Almost all fabric benefits from wet-finishing, except for some rugs, art weaves, and a few that only require steaming or ironing. Except for the rag projects, all projects in this book need wet-finishing. The results can be dramatic. For lace weaves, wet-finishing is essential to bring out the lace effect. Wet-finish your samples to avoid unwelcome surprises later. Fabric right off the loom is often stiff. Once wet,

threads relax and the fabric resolves. The first washing sets the cloth and results in the most shrinkage. If wrinkled and the fabric is allowed to dry at this stage, these wrinkles may never come out. When almost dry, iron and finish according to the fiber and fabric content. Hand wash **wool** in cool to warm water—never hot—with little or no agitation. (A combination of heat, water, and agitation can produce unwanted **felt**.) Put a little pH-neutral soap, like Orvus™, dissolved in cool to warm water; place flat in water. Soap encourages threads to slip together. A few tablespoons of liquid Wisk™ in the water will remove mill oil and sizing. Leave fabric in the water for at least an hour without disturbing it until it completely absorbs water. Drain, pull fabric aside, and refill for a thorough rinse with cool water. Drain, squeeze (but never twist), and roll up in a towel. Block and hang until the weaving is almost dry. Steam thoroughly on both sides and trim threads. With mixed fibers in a fabric always select the fiber that is the most sensitive to finishing and proceed in this manner.

Silk likes warm water. If the water or iron is too hot, fibers can become damaged even if it doesn't show. Wash as above, but if added crispness is desired, give it a double rinse—the first with a few tablespoons of white vinegar. For fine silk that seems to float in air: put it in the dryer, check every few minutes until there is a sudden change from heavy and wet to light and feathery. At that point, take it from the dryer and iron it dry.

Cotton can take hot water and soaping. Finish the same as wool, but with hot water. Mercerized cotton will shrink less than unmercerized cotton. **Cottolin** is a mixture of cotton and linen, so finish it as you would cotton.

Linen loves abuse. What we don't dare to do to other fibers, we can do to linen. Run a tub filled with the hottest water out of the pipes. Put the cloth flat into the water, being careful not to twist or wrinkle it. Leave it for a long while until cool, even overnight. Roll it in a towel to absorb as much moisture as possible, then iron it dry. Dry-spun linen is beautiful, but tends to shed, so I recommend using a dust mask when weaving it. Newer linen thread may be brittle because of the use of chemicals to break it down. Make a linen warp, tie it, and then simmer it at a *very low* temperature on the stove for an hour, changing the water several times. When the water stays clear, rinse and hang to dry. If linen is woven in a dry environment it can break, so you may wish to make a

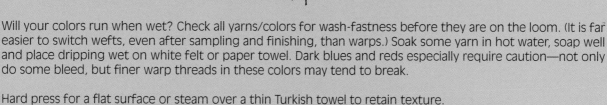

Will your colors run when wet? Check all yarns/colors for wash-fastness before they are on the loom. (It is far easier to switch wefts, even after sampling and finishing, than warps.) Soak some yarn in hot water, soap well and place dripping wet on white felt or paper towel. Dark blues and reds especially require caution—not only do some bleed, but finer warp threads in these colors may tend to break.

Hard press for a flat surface or steam over a thin Turkish towel to retain texture.

linen dressing of 20 parts water to one part flax seed, available at health food stores. Simmer the mixture until thick and sieve to remove seeds. Enter the warp and let it steep off heat for an hour or so. Run your hands down the warp to remove excess and hang to dry. (Extra flax dressing can be stored in a marked canning jar.) Even though this is a messy process, once it is dry, the treated linen acts just like silk.

If further strengthening is needed on the loom while weaving, spray the warp with water three times, 10 minutes apart. When the yarn feels warm, you know it is ready. Continue to spray every time you advance the warp, especially at the heddles. Soak bobbins that carry linen weft, using one and then the other as they dry. When the warp looks light against the weft, it is time to spray the warp; when the weft looks light against the warp, it is time to rotate the bobbin. Rub some lanolin on the loom and metal parts to protect them.

Raise Nap on a Fabric (with wool, mohair, or similar fibers): During the first wetting, brush with a natural bristle brush in the direction of the warp and weft on one or both sides, taking care not to catch any skips. You may want to brush just one side so that one side is informal, the other side more formal.

Storage: After finishing, a good way to handle fabric is to roll it up on a tube. If you store handwovens for any period of time, wrap them around an acid-free tube or one lined with acid free paper. Check and rotate regularly.

High-Fashion Garments

Ingrid Boesel, Master Weaver from Guelph, Ontario, Canada designed and sewed these runway-ready garments.

"Flames" dress, warp of 32 colors in cotton with lilac wefts in cottons, Quigley—single 4-tie weave.

"Poppies," kimono-style coat, warp of 35 colors with black weft in cottons—original pattern with unusual supplementary warp weave on 16 shafts.

6 Knots and Other Tricks of the Trade

Peter Collingwood's "SS-30" is a shaft-switched rug of horsehair and wool, 38" x 76".

Knots are essential for warping and weaving. Chances are you are already familiar with some or all of these. Those used in this book are shown on the next page in two colors, since most use two or more strands. It's also useful to try other knots and combinations to find what works best for you.

Basic Knots

The overhand knot.

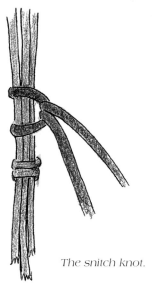

The snitch knot.

1 The **overhand knot**, also called the **circle knot**, is useful for changing colors while making a warp, tying each thread of a new warp onto a previous warp, and many other repeating fast-action weaving tasks.

With your right hand, twist two threads to the right (clockwise) until they form a circle with the right end on top; pull the ends through from the back and pull tight. If only one end comes through the circle, the knot will not hold.

3 The **snitch knot** is really two knots working together: the overhand knot and the lark's head. This knot holds bundled yarns securely, yet is easily released by relaxing the tension on the lark's head. Bundle a series of threads with an overhand knot toward the ends and catch them up with a lark's head above the knot. Looping over the bundle, then pulling the ends through the loop makes the lark's head.

The square knot.

The slip knot.

2 The **square knot** is stronger than the overhand knot. Use this knot any time you wish to secure two threads together that will "sit tight" under great tension.

Twist one thread around the other, loop both threads over the top, twist them again in the opposite direction, and pull tight. A stronger variation is to twist twice around one direction, then twice the other direction, and pull tight.

4 The **slip knot** secures two or more threads together temporarily and releases with just a tug on the loop ends. It secures groups of threads, for example, through the reed and heddles. This is the same motion used to begin to chain a warp.

Loop the yarns in a circle and pull just the loop through. If the ends pull through, the knot will become permanent.

Basic Skills

1. To Tie Warp Ends on the Rod on the Front of the Loom: I work out of the reed, each hand picking up threads in three or four reed dents at a time. *I do not count threads; I count reed dents.* This is fast and makes the right size bundles no matter what size threads you are using at what sett. The bundles are small so the weaving becomes established quickly.

Begin with the outside bundle on each side. With half the threads in each hand, pull each group up from under the stick or rod. Cross the groups at the center and bring them under and around. Coming up from around the outside, pull up and tension by *pushing away* from your body using your thumbs as leverage, perhaps wiggling the group side to side, and over-tie. Re-tie across. Next, from the center out, tension evenly by adjusting each tie. Repeat from the *outside in and center out* until the tension is perfectly even when you pat your hand across the threads. End from the inside out and over-tie again to hold. Tie the very last bundle on each side last and extra tight, then move them in slightly to compensate for draw-in as the weaving begins. (Some people also split this last group in half for greater edge control.) This full knot releases easily by tugging on one set of the knotted threads.

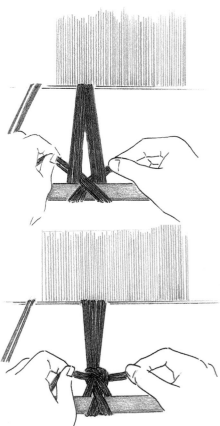

Cross threads from 3-4 reed dents each (top); over-tie (bottom). NOTE: Some weavers make each bundle into an overhand knot, then lace through them with a cord around a rod at the front, adjusting the cord across for even tension. For this system to work, the bundles must be small.

2. To Tie in a Warp Thread: Should a thread break in the warp, locate the broken thread. Tie a new thread onto it, long enough to hang over the back of the loom a few inches, and slip the broken thread out of the reed and heddle to the back, pulling the new thread through with it. Clip the broken thread from the new thread. Tie the new end in at the fell of the cloth with a pin in a figure 8 and bury the tip in the cloth. Hang a light weight on the new thread over the back (such as a light-weight chain from a hardware store or fishing weights). After weaving a few inches, tie the end of the broken thread to the new thread and pull it back through the heddle and reed. Clip the substitute and tie the original thread in with a pin as a figure 8. When the cloth is off the loom, with a large-eye blunt needle, carefully run these threads in and out of the weaving, overlapping according to weave structure in the warp direction. After wet-finishing, clip to the cloth. Should you encounter a knot in the warp, clip the knot and proceed as above.

3. To Tie in a Repair Heddle: If you skip a thread when warping, there are several options.

(A) Take a strong thread (I reuse linen thrums) and, with half the thread each side, tie a lark's head knot on top over the bar on the shaft where the missing heddle is needed. Tie an overhand knot at about the center of the thread, tugging it up exactly to the top of the eye of the other heddles. Tie another overhand knot exactly at the bottom of the eye of the other heddles, tie around the bottom bar with a square knot, and trim the ends.

(B) If using System Texsolv heddles, put the new heddle around the top bar and through the heddles above the eyes to the insertion point, then put the bottom through below the eyes and around the bottom bar. Adjust. This works better if you bunch the heddles to the insertion

Tie in a repair heddle using strong thread.

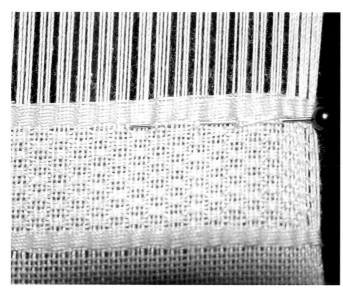

Tie the new end in at the fell of the cloth with a pin in a figure 8 and bury the tip in the cloth.

point and if there is sufficient room between the shafts.

(C) With two extra metal heddles, place one in front of the top and bottom bars and the other behind both bars at the insertion point. Line up so the eye of both shows through. Tie the top and bottom of both heddles to the bars with thread and put the warp end through both as one. If you have only one heddle, do the same, but use bread ties to secure it to the top and bottom bars.

(D) Buy a metal repair heddle with clasps at the top and bottom that slip over each bar.

4. Hemstitching: A precise and beautiful method for anchoring the edges of handweaving, it not only holds with most fibers, but also gives a nice finish. It is useful for items that are fringed, not hemmed, as it is less bulky than knots.

Linen is an exception when used at the edges of an item, since both the hemstitching and the fringe will, with repeated washings, wear away. Linen can, however, be hemstitched within the body of the cloth. (Right-handers follow the photos; lefties may work from the left and reverse the process.)

(A) **Hemstitching at the Beginning of Weaving:** Leave a tail of weft hanging out the right side, three times the width of the warp for finer hemstitching or four times for heavier threads. Put in at least three picks of weft. Loosen the warp one notch.

Decide how many threads to group and how many rows to go into the cloth to anchor them. *Count out of the reed,* from two to four reed dents

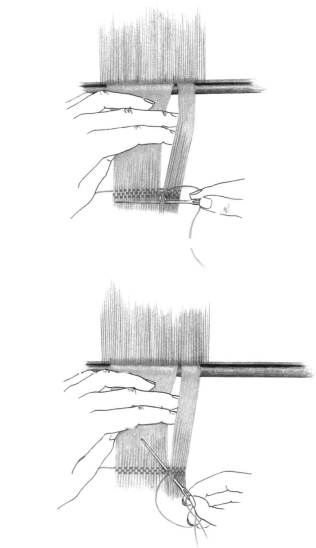

Hemstitching at the beginning of weaving.

and from two to three rows. Here I selected two reed dents—two warp threads to work around. I also elected to work *around* and up into two rows of the woven cloth. The left hand separates the warp so the fingers work out of the reed, which makes it easy to see where to place the needle.

Using a blunt needle, go around the outside of the right edge, coming up under two reed dents into the space below. Then place the needle around again, but now two picks up into the cloth. This is at the same vertical spacing (two reed dents, two threads). Next, the needle goes down in that same

> ### Hint
> Use a blunt needle and take care to never split a warp thread.

vertical row below (the one last used) and comes up into the next vertical space across as before (two more reed dents). The needle next goes down between the previous vertical space and comes up between the second and third row where the needle began (two reed dents, two threads); pull very tight. Repeat across, giving a quick tug at the bottom and top turns.

End with a loop and slip the needle downward so the hemstitched thread becomes part of the fringe. Tighten up to the cloth. If it is the same color and weight, it is invisible.

(B) **Hemstitching at the End of Weaving:** Follow the directions as before, but where the needle was working around the threads from underneath up into the cloth *above*, now it is working around the threads and from underneath up into the cloth *below*. End with a loop and slip the needle upward so it becomes part of that fringe.

See the last photo in Chapter 13 (on page 135) that shows hemstitching after finishing with the little holes that develop from this technique.

Hemstitching at the end of weaving.

Slit Wedge Weave Rugs

Martha Stanley of Watsonville, California has taken Navajo Wedge Weave to new heights. Her agate-color blends integrated with effective slits that set off her designs are noteworthy.

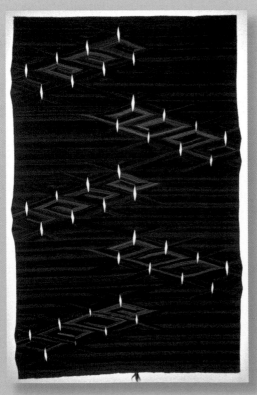

Slit Wedge Weave rug is woven with four selvedges, 46" x 72" and 5 feet x 8 feet.

Essentials for the New Weaver: A First Project

Mini-runners: one in two colors, hemstiched with fringe, and the other hemmed.

It's time to plan and weave your first project. This is also a chance for weavers with some experience and study groups to review.

Get organized. Keep a running detailed account of your weaving experiences in a notebook. You may think you'll remember every detail forever, but those details vanish with the next project. Write down everything—what you like and what you don't, what goes right and what goes wrong. Periodically re-copy your notes to clarify and review. You will find your notes invaluable—perhaps a favorite yarn in a sample you love, a color you excluded, the reed that worked,

Each project in this book is a vehicle for a set of lessons. Consider each project a beginning point rather than a recipe. Original designs are always preferred. Whenever you can, modify an idea and make it your own. Be brave. Try new things and discover why some ideas work, some work better, and some don't work at all. Change the yarn or size, surrender to a special fiber and color you like, combine various sizes and colors in new ways. On each warp, weave a sample and try new treadlings. You may like yours best.

or a special draft to weave again. Label all yarns with fiber, brand and source, size and dye lot, date, and any other known information such as cost. After using, add the sett and weave to the project notes.

NOTE: This project is woven on a table loom, but you can also weave it on *any* floor loom. Bobbin shuttles work well with this weight and type of yarn, but you can use *any* suitable shuttle.

Before you can plan a project, you must understand take-up and loom waste.

Warp Take-Up: As the weft is woven into the warp and beaten into place, the warp "takes up," or rolls over and under each weft. Heavy wefts (such as rug yarns) produce more warp take-up than finer yarns. Weave structure also affects the amount of take-up. The more the warp interlaces with the weft, the greater the take-up; the more the warp skips over wefts, the less the take-up. Because take-up shortens

a warp, you must plan this into each project. In this project, all yarns interlace with all others in plain weave, but they are relatively small yarns.

Weft Take-Up: The weft also has take-up because it must travel over and under each warp. In addition, the weft catches the selvedge which tends to move the edge in, called **draw-in**. Consequently, a weaving 10" wide in the reed may, like this one, become 9" wide while weaving on the loom and, after wet-finishing, become 8" wide. Always expect some draw-in unless you use a temple (shown in use in Chapter 11 on page 114). As edge threads move closer, a stronger wearing edge results.

Loom waste is warp left on the loom after the project is cut off. To minimize the length of these **thrums**, "scotch" the warp by weaving until the rod holding the end of the warp is right at the back of the heddles. A table loom generally has less loom waste than a floor loom because table looms are usually not as deep. In general, figure a half yard loom waste into a table loom project and one yard loom waste for a floor loom.

For overall design, work out placement and proportion of colors or textures, then select an appropriate weave structure. A free-form design put into a profile draft is an excellent approach to this type of designing. Another approach is a thread-by-thread draft, a design already in a particular weave structure; plain weave is the selection here. Use book and magazine references for inspiration—*Handwoven* magazine from Interweave Press is especially noted for its attractive beginner through intermediate projects.

Inspirational Scarf and Shawl

Mary Bentley of Bowen Island, British Columbia, Canada, is celebrated for her use of spontaneous color in multi-shaft weaving, having spent 12 years focusing on this technique. Here are two polychrome "Summer-and-Winter" silk weavings.

"Antigua Dreams," 16-shaft with pickup.

"Bowen Maples," 16-shaft scarf.

Mini-Runner #1 and #2

Mini-Runner #2 in two colors, hemstitched with fringe. Mini-Runner #1 in dark teal, hemmed.

Project Plans:

This project lets you practice reading a draft for a simple weave structure: balanced plain weave on two shafts. Make the warp, dress the loom, and weave a hemmed mini-runner in one color or one hemstitched in two colors. Both projects use a one-color warp.

Get specific. Before you can make a warp, you must decide what to weave, what yarn to use, and what color you will be using.

How can you tell if a yarn is suitable for warp? It is not how easily yarn breaks from pulling that determines this, rather how easily it breaks from abrasion. Test by rubbing your fingernail hard back and forth on a yarn. (For example, 8/4 carpet warp, used frequently for rug weaving, breaks readily when pulled, but resists abrasion well.) Weft need not be strong.

Warp calculations are exact. Once you know how many yards you need for your project and how many yards there are in each pound, you can figure how many pounds (or ounces) you need for warp. Suppliers can tell you yardage for their yarns and may have charts of common setts for standard yarn sizes in some structures. This can help you estimate yardage for a given project. The Yarn Chart in this book includes yardage estimates for many standard yarns (see Chapter 5, page 59). If yardage is unknown, get a close estimate with the McMorran Yarn Balance.

Weft calculations are not exact. I've tried various formulas, but found none applicable to a variety of weaves. Mills use mathematically complex formulas. Weft usage varies with structure and sett, yarn characteristics, number of warp-weft interlacements, etc. Each weaver warps and weaves with a different "hand"—how tightly the warp is made and rolled on, how heavily the fabric is beaten, how much draw-in results. Each loom, too, varies in how it handles. Even the same yarn size varies from mill to mill. With two or more weft yarns, the figuring becomes more complicated. With so many variables, it is impractical to consider every one.

To calculate weft for any 50/50 balanced weave project of all the same size yarns, such as this project and others in this book, figure the same amount of weft yarn as warp yarn. This allows for weaving as much of the warp as possible, taking into account loom waste, take-up, and shrinkage.

Plan the Warp for Mini-Runner #1: How much warp does this project require? This table loom is 10" wide in the reed, so let's plan a runner 10" wide. For a balanced weave, 3/2 cotton setts at 12 epi. Multiply 10" by 12 cpi equalling 120 total warp ends. Determine the length of the sample and the runner, add in take-up and loom waste, and consider shrinkage. Since the runner is 8" wide after draw-in and finishing, a simple proportion that works is to make a runner **3** x 8 = a finished length of 24" long. Warp shrinkage for Mini-Runner #1 is expected to be approximately 15 percent, so weave it 3" to 4" longer equalling 28". Add another ½ yard for take-up and loom waste on a table loom equals 18". Add 2" at each end for hems equalling 4". The total so far is 50". Allow 12" for sampling, to cut off and wet-finish, and tie back on equalling another ½ yard. This total is over 2 yards, so round up to 2½ yards.

Plan the Weft: Multiply 120 warps by 2½ yards equalling 300 yards of warp. Since you use the same yarn for weft in this 50/50 weave, plan 300 yards weft.

Plan the Warp for Mini-Runner #2: This runner has fringe, so weave a heading of one inch at both ends to anchor the fringe. Insert two 2" cardboard spacers at each end for fringe equalling 4". The total fringe is 10". To the total warp above of 2½ yards we add this 10", round up to 3 yards; Multiply 120 by 3 yards equalling 360 yards for warp (color 1).

Plan the Weft: Select a color that is closely related, such as a darker or lighter color than the warp, as here. For this 50/50 weave, plan the same amount of weft as warp: 360 yards.

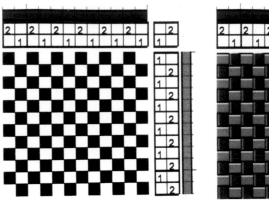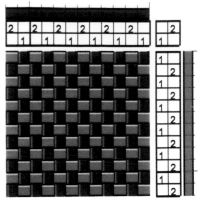

Structural draft (left) and color-and-weave-effect draft (right). The first two threads in the warp make up one repeat; the first two picks in the weft make up one repeat. Each is repeated as indicated for the entire project.

NOTE: A whole pound of 3/2 yarn is 1,260 yd./lb. and is more than you need for either runner. However, some suppliers will sell mini-cones or wind some off for you.

PROJECT LAYOUT:

Project	Mini-Runner #1: one color warp and weft, hemmed; or Mini-Runner #2: one color warp, another related color weft, hemstitched
Equipment	Loom with two (or more) shafts
Structure	Plain weave
Yarns and Colors	Project #1 is of 3/2 yarn at 1260 yd./lb. cotton in one color for warp and weft; Project #2 is of 3/2 cotton yarns – one color for warp, a second color for weft
Sett	12 epi, one per dent in a 12 dpi reed or 2 per dent in a 6 (see Sett Chart on page 43 for others)
Width in Reed	10"
Make Warp	120 threads x 2½ yards for #1 =300 yards, 120 threads x 3 yards for #2 = 360 yards
Estimate Weft	Approximately the same amount of weft will be needed, 300 yards for #1 of the same color, or 360 yards for #2 of a second color.

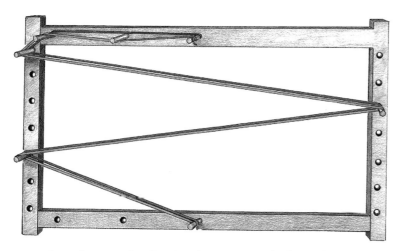

The red yarn is the direction the warp travels down the warping board; the green yarn is the direction it travels up.

Make the Warp on a Warping Board:
You can make a warp various ways (with a warping mill, pegs clamped on a table, etc.), but a warping board is ideal for this project as it is stable and can be mounted on a wall. This method is easy to learn, quick, and efficient. The warping board shown at left is one yard across and can make up to 14½ yards of warp. Make your warp, depending on which project you chose, either 2½ or 3 yards long (as shown here) x 120 ends. Yarns on the board move a half yard across the top and bottom (equals 1 yard) plus 2 yards straight across equals 3 yards altogether. Warps can often be made with two or more yarns at a time, but for this project, use just one yarn.

Making the Warp

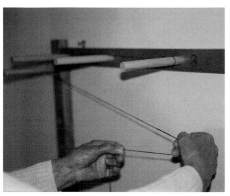

1. **Begin Making the Warp:** *Tie the yarn on the first peg at the top center right. Continue left over all the other top pegs.*

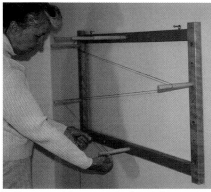

2. *Draw out the yarn to the right over the peg on the right at the same time the left hand draws out the yarn to the left, over the peg on the left. Continue to the bottom and repeat the same pattern on the way up.*

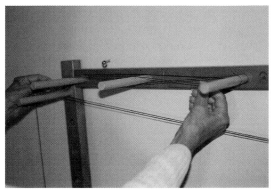

3. *Dip the yarn under the center peg to make the weaver's cross.*

The Weaver's Cross: Some say weaving could not have been accomplished efficiently until the invention of a way to keep all the yarns in order. The weaver's cross is important because it does just that. Yarns go over a peg in one direction and under a peg in the other, in a figure 8 fashion. *(You can go over a peg in one direction and under on return as here, or vice-versa, but you must be consistent.)*

Begin Warp: To learn, an optional leader yarn in two colors can be made of the first round on a warping board, one down and one up, to mark the path of the warp, but is not part of it. Keep the leader yarn on the board until you are sure of the sequence.

Warping: Mount the board so you can reach the top pegs comfortably and just barely look down at the top yarns. Stand at the center of the warping board and place your yarn centered below on the floor, on a holding peg if possible. Always pull the yarn up at the center, then right or left, so there is minimal pull at each side of the package. The warp yarn is tied on the first peg at the top center right, goes left over all the other top pegs, and from the center of the board, the right hand draws out the yarn to the right over the peg on the right *at the same time* the left hand draws out the yarn to the left over the peg on the left. Repeat this process until you reach the bottom center peg where it turns to go up. On the way up, repeat the same process with hands drawing out from the center, but also, where the yarn turns the side pegs, push these yarns back. As you reach the top, dip the yarn under the center peg to make the weaver's cross. Repeat.

NOTE: Yarns going from top to bottom go around and *down* each side peg. Yarns going from bottom to top go around and *up* each side peg.

Make the warp with a light hand, tension even. Always place the working yarn in front of the previous strand, not over it. At any time you need to stop during warping, as when counting yarns, wrap the yarn around and over itself on a peg to hold it in place. End by tying on the peg where you began.

Walking the Dog

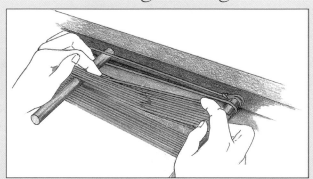

"Walking the dog" is the best and fastest way to count yarns as you warp. Place one hand on each side of the cross with the fingers around only the top set of yarns. The left finger pulls the top yarns forward, releasing the yarn on the opposite side.

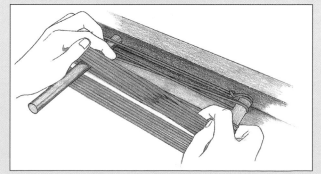

Then the right finger pulls all the top yarns, releasing the yarn on the other side. Each hand alternates as you count. Yarns should have some tension. If sticky, your fingers can push the released yarn away.

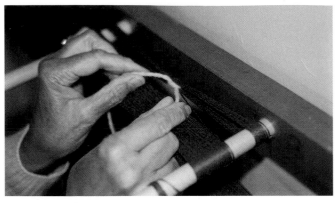

4. Tie the cross: as you are "walking the dog," you may wish to tie a heavy yarn at the cross around groups in the warp of whatever repeat you select

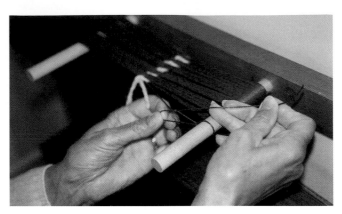

5A. This warp is tied with white yarn in six groups of 20 yarns each.

5B. If you do not need to count the warp by groups, you can tie a yarn around all the threads at the cross.

5C. If you need to stabilize or store the warp, add extra ties.

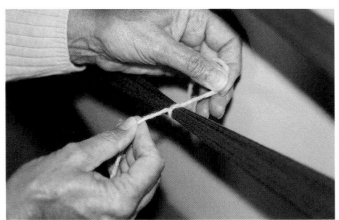

6. It is always good to make a choke tie at the center of each yard and at the end. This tie can be any that releases, tight enough to keep the warp in order and keep it from tangling.

7. The warp is tied and ready to chain.

8. Chain the warp: release the warp at the bottom center peg and begin to chain.

9. Put your hand through the end loops, grasp the warp a little higher, and pull it through to form a new loop.

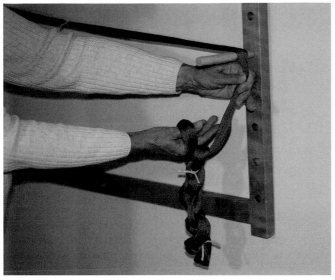

10. Chain all the way to the top, tensioning against the pegs of the warping board so the yarns don't slip off the pegs prematurely.

11. Slip the last chained loop at the top over a peg on the left, hands free until the cross is secured.

12. Place a lease stick in each side of the cross; on the right also slide the loops from the beginning and end of the warp, from the peg onto the stick with the rest of the warp—these loops make it easy to find the first and last yarns when you begin to warp the loom.

13. Tie the lease sticks together through end holes so you can't lose the cross, and tie the end loop of the chain to one of the lease sticks so the chaining will not come undone.

Warping the Loom Front to Back

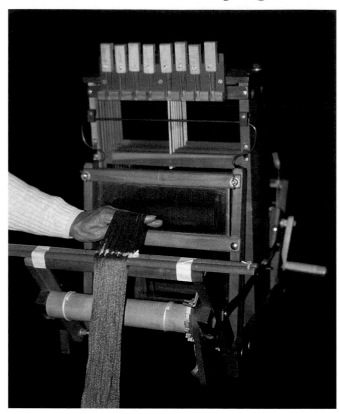

1. **Begin Warping the Loom:** *Dress the loom front to back. Using this method, you can warp any loom 10" or wider for this project. You could also warp back to front as shown in the next chapter. Carry the lease sticks that hold the cross to the table loom. Loosely attach them to the front beam with masking or painter's tape at the sides. (Yarn may also be used if the sticks do not slip.)*

2. *The first and last threads of the warp are tied at the ends of the lease sticks. Remove all ties, keeping the cross. Pull the yarns out gently so as not to lose the cross.*

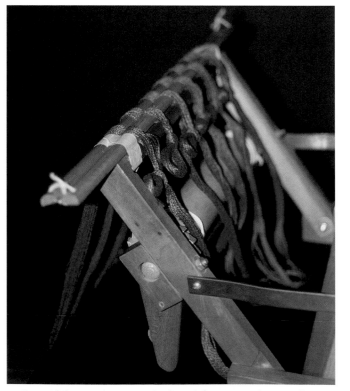

3. *Cut the ends.*

4. *Spread the warp across in the sticks, over-tying or slip knotting each section of 20 threads.*

On a Wider Loom

A. Center the warp in the reed: there are 120 yarns total in this warp sett at 12 epi (120 divided by 12 equals 10" which is the width of this reed, so you'll use almost every dent in the reed). But what if the reed is wider than the warp? To center the warp in a wider reed, use this fast and foolproof method that uses no numbers. Let a measuring tape "do the thinking" for you. Lay the measuring tape the length of the reed and place your right thumbnail at the reed end, in this case the reed is 24" wide. Place your left thumbnail at the width of the project, in this case 10".

B. Fold over the tape measure, nail to nail; this cuts the measurement in half.

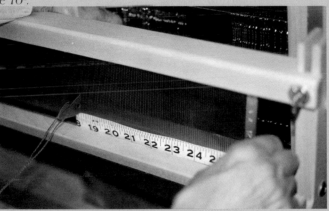

C. Place the folded end at the right end of the reed. The tape ends on the left exactly where denting begins, where the reed hook is seen ready to sley the first warp thread in the reed.

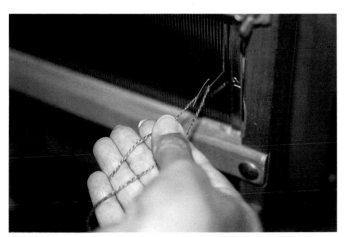

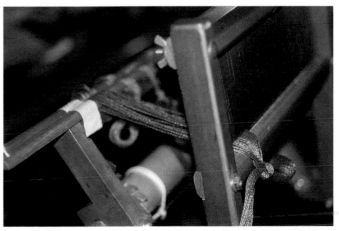

5. **Sley the Reed:** Working out of the lease sticks on the table loom, right to left in order, sley one yarn in each dent of a 12 reed with a reed hook. Some looms have a way to secure the reed/beater between the front beam and the shafts to stabilize it. If not, rest your upper arm on the top of the reed for balance and sley it with your other hand.

6. Bundle behind the reed by 20s.

7. Thread one yarn in each heddle, following the order in the lease sticks from right to left. Since this is plain weave on 2 shafts, put the first yarn in the first heddle on the shaft closest to the front of the loom. Put the next yarn in the first heddle on the second shaft. These 2 yarns are one repeat of the structure. Repeat across.

8. Tie each bundle of 20 behind the heddles with a slip knot to secure them.

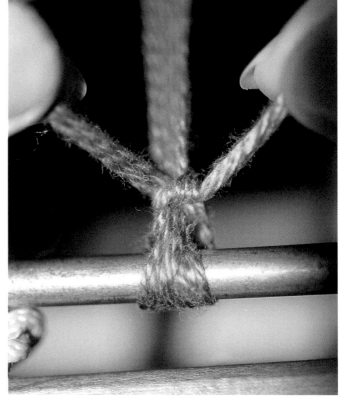

9. Ready to roll: Remove lease sticks. Gently pull each bundle to the back and tie it onto the back rod.

10. You can tie on almost any way you like as long as the groups are relatively small, the ends about even, the groups of warp ends approximately the same in number, and the knot firm (this is my preferred method).

Thread the Heddles: Check to see you have enough heddles on each shaft; if not, add them now. If there are too many, remove extras as you see here, or tie them back to the side out of the way. It is a good idea to bundle threads and heddles as you work. For example, this warp is tied in groups of 20, so bundle threads and heddles by 20. The warp is threaded alternately on 1 and 2, so move over 10 heddles on shaft 1, and 10 on shaft 2. When done threading, the number of threads and heddles used should come out the same; if not, check for a threading error. It is easiest to correct one now. Repeat across. This becomes even more important in threading complex weaves, block weaves, and drafts with more shafts.

11. The rod must come over the back beam.

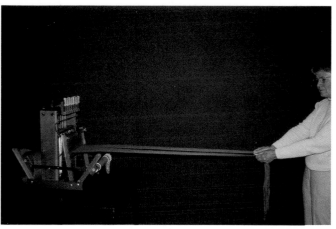

12. From the front, comb out the warp with your fingers; give it a shake and a tug. Ideally the yarns should all be lined up evenly, but don't count on it. The farther back you stand, the easier it is to straighten out the warp. Comb and strum the warp like a guitar to get rid of snarls.

To Beam or Roll on the Warp: Wind the warp on the back beam while turning the crank on the back beam. (Check to be sure you turn it the correct direction. The brake must hold fast one direction until the break is released; the warp fills in the other direction.) I prefer to warp alone. Insert a piece of corrugated cardboard, long enough to go around the back beam at least once, covering the knots. (The best has wales on only one side. It will tend to flatten with repeated use—if new and you use it throughout, it could vary the tension until broken in.) After one turn over the knots, tuck ordinary brown paper inside about the width of the back beam. If you run out, tuck another piece inside and repeat. (Don't use newspaper, as it leaves oily residue.) You can use yardsticks or slats from blinds if you put at least one in every turn; these fall out when weaving later. Any of these methods will help keep the warp even, preventing yarns from slipping into previous rows.

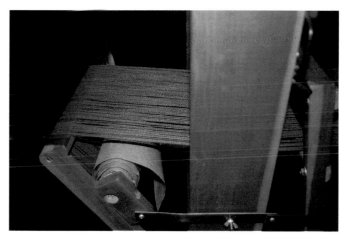

13. Pull the warp at the front in small handfuls to tension evenly across, then drop. Turn the handle on the crank, once around. Repeat until the warp is all rolled on. Leave about 4" hanging from the front beam. Cut the ends of the warp evenly across and slip knot bundle them so they can't slip through the reed.

TIPS

While rolling on the warp, put the beater forward against the front beam so if yarn snags in the reed, it will move the reed back as you crank and warn you to stop and shake out the warp again. You don't want any warp yarns to catch and break. If it is hard to roll the threads on at any point, stop and check across the heddles as well as the reed for a snarl or twisted thread. For sticky warps, raise half the shafts while rolling on; this does not disturb the tension. If needed to help glide on easier, spread a washable oil conditioner on a wool warp or use an anti-static spray on silk. If threads tend to twist around each other, keep more tension on these threads.

Weavers around the World

Men in Guatemala usually weave on floor looms, while women weave on backstrap looms.

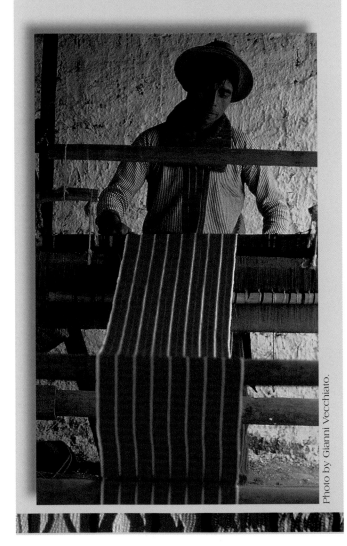

Photo by Gianni Vecchiato.

Even Tension: Perhaps the biggest concern for a new weaver is to put on a warp with even tension. Take heart... this improves with every warp. If there is someone available to hold the warp while you turn the back beam and roll it on, you can roll it on under tension. However, I generally don't recommend this because, even with a warp as narrow as this, each handful of yarns forms a "v." Winding on at that angle may produce uneven tension as the edge yarns tend to be longer and later selvedges slacken. Whatever

method you use, aim for even tension throughout the warp.

Some warping considerations: (A) One person should make the warp and one person should roll it on so there is no difference in tension across the warp; (B) many warps shrink more in the warp direction than in the weft direction—keep measurements at each stage and compare on-loom, off-loom, and after finishing; and (C) it's better to have too much warp on the loom than too little.

Let's Weave Magic: There are various ways to tie on the front beam. I prefer the same knot on the front rod as on the back (see pages 64 and 76). After tying on the front, crank any slack at the back and then adjust the tension at the front—usually a ratchet or two more. Cotton requires a bit more tension than wool, linen a bit more than cotton, fine threads more than medium threads. The warp must not be so soft it sags, but tight enough that it snaps back when you "pop" the edges. If the edge is taut, you will weave with an even selvedge because each time the weft catches at the edge, it can fully recover to its previous width. If you over-tension, some shafts may sit higher or you may not be able to lift them easily.

Problem Checks: Push down on lever 1 on the table loom to lift shaft 1; then release it and push down on lever 2 to lift shaft 2. Look at each shed from the side. If each shed is a clear "v" in front of and behind the beater, you're home free. If not, correct it now.

(A) If one or more yarns are crossed or in the wrong heddles, correct by putting them back into sequence. Let's guess you threaded 1212211; you need to switch the two underlined threads to 1212121.

(B) Perhaps you skipped a heddle in the sequence or put a thread on the wrong shaft. Let's say you threaded 121-121, the 2 is missing. There is no extra heddle to use. Since you don't want to rethread them all from that point across, you can make a "repair heddle" and add it into the sequence on shaft 2 (see Chapter 5, page 65).

(C) You may have too many yarns in one dent or may have skipped some dents. Redent now to avoid **reed marks**, warp-wise lines, or spaces in cloth that don't wash out.

This checklist sounds like a lot can go wrong, but actually these problems are all easily rectified. Remember, if you count and tie bundles and count and move heddles as you thread, very few errors occur that are not quickly correctable. You may cut yarns

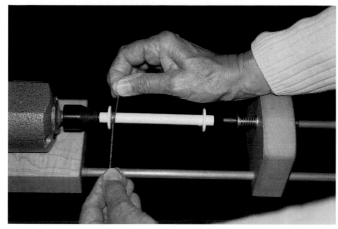

1. *Whatever equipment you use, wind the thread around the bobbin once and then twist it back in the reverse direction, holding it steady so it doesn't slip, until the thread begins to fill over it. Don't tie the thread on the bobbin because, when it runs out, it will catch and disrupt the edge.*

2. *Hold the yarn under light tension and feed it along the length of the bobbin at an angle by keeping it moving left and right, but never go backwards over a previous thread; build a "hill" at each end, and a "smile" that dips in the center.*

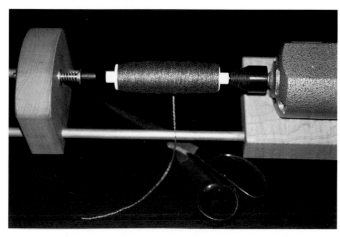

3. *Continue, gradually moving in from the end until the "hills" are level with the ends, then fill the center area back and forth until it is level with the top of the shuttle when inserted.*

close to the front for corrections and knot on a longer length if necessary—this is permitted at the start of the weaving.

Fill Bobbins: It is slow winding a bobbin by hand, so some apparatus is preferable, especially for fine threads. Photos show an electric winder holding the bobbin at both ends. You can also use a power drill or build your own using a variety of parts including a sewing machine motor.

Weave your Sample: I use bath tissue to spread the warp. Place one length of tissue in the first shed, then change the shed and beat. Place a second length in that shed, change the shed, place another length in that shed, and beat both. Beat in this manner several more times until the warp is spaced evenly across.

NOTE: some looms have an optional shuttle race, a ledge at the base of the beater, as an assist with the lower shed as the shuttle moves across. You can weave equally well with or without one.

Weave several inches of each color. Cut from the loom and slip knot the warp to safeguard it. Keep figures for your sample: on the loom, off-loom, and after wet-finishing. Wet-finish as planned for the weaving—see details later in the chapter. Don't worry, washing can't ruin your weaving; actually it turns threads into fabric, increases drape, and improves its appearance.

Things to Remember as You Weave

1. Always place the bobbin in the shuttle so the yarn comes from under the bobbin and out the side. Always weave with the hole in the bobbin shuttle toward you.
2. If the yarn on the bobbins gets too drawn out, wind it up under tension by using alternate thumbs on the shuttle.

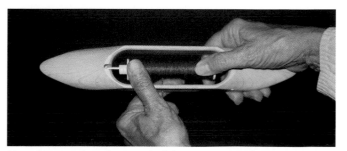

Use alternate thumbs to wind the yarn up under tension.

1. Hold the shuttle as shown. Flex your wrist. Throw the shuttle through the shed, across the warp. Strength comes from the wrist guided by the first two fingers.

2. Catch the shuttle with the other hand and lift it just above the beater, straight up without turning it, until you feel the yarn catch the edge of the weaving. With thumb on top, and sometimes also fingers under the shuttle, stop the bobbin from unwinding. From the center of the beater, flick the wrist slightly sideways to beat. Change the shed and beat again to clear the shed for the next throw. The shuttle is in position to throw again, in line with the reed. Lower it to shed level and throw. NOTE: the yarn lies on top of the bottom warp yarns as a diagonal line, beginning where it was last beaten in and ending at the reed on the other side.

3. When the cloth turns around the cloth beam the first time, insert a piece of corrugated cardboard, or other very heavy paper, at least several inches more than the width of the weaving, to cover the knots so they can't disrupt the tension. This is easy to forget, but important.

4. Each loom is a little different. Find the two-inch area where the beater hits nearest to a right angle with the cloth. Weave within this area. Move the warp often, about every inch or so. (Each loom advances differently; release the warp on the back beam and wind the warp up at the front.) Write or print out the treadling and attach it to the loom, such as with wax clips. A simple method to keep track of where you are in the treadling, seen in antique drafts with pinholes, is to stick a pin in the paper and move it as you advance.

Beat: The standard sequence is a syncopated throw, beat, change, beat on an open shed. Even with a light beat, you should hear a small snap when the beater hits the fell of the cloth. Shed changing is easier with a floor loom, since treadles don't interrupt the rhythm. You may have to put down the shuttle to change the shed if you are on a table loom. Use a standard medium beat with this project. The weft should move up right close to the previous row, but not touch it; the following pick will move the previous pick in just a bit. Try various beats with your sample, then wet-finish to decide what looks and feels best.

The term "beat" can be a misnomer since, with light-weight cloth, the beater can be used just to place the yarn, or bring the yarn up to the previous yarn without beating. Sometimes a single harder beat, or a double beat, is used, especially with rugs. You can beat on a closed shed—no shed, no active shafts—but that is harder on edge yarns. It is helpful, however,

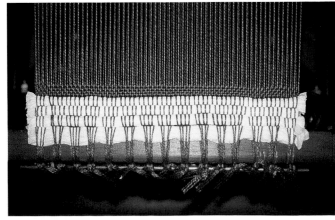

The warp tied on, spread out with bath tissue, and a few picks woven in.

The sample woven with both colors.

looms for working height. Fortunately, many looms come apart to make it easy to access various parts of the loom as you work.

Sit over the warp, relaxed so your elbows are just above the warp. When you throw the shuttle, never lift your shoulders or involve any of your body except your hands, elbows, and arms. There should be no tension or stress anywhere, especially in your wrists. It takes very little motion to snap the beater and snap the shuttle across. It's not how hard you do it, but how effectively. Never pull the beater toward you with both arms, as it stretches the chest and throws the shoulders back—use your wrist instead. Never squeeze the beater against the fell line, just snap it. After you get into a rhythm, check to see if any part of your body is struggling. You may rock back and forth slightly to the rhythm, especially with overhead beaters, which sometimes require holding the beater back to enlarge the shed for the shuttle. Lean side-to-side for a wide warp and stretch your legs for treadles, but keep all motion to a minimum—flowing and relaxed. You want to weave cloth, not wear yourself out.

when weft is very wiry. Sometimes a weaving needs a varied beat throughout. Try beat variations when standard methods don't achieve desired results. Begin with traditional methods, but be willing to experiment.

Ergonomics: Much of weaving involves repetitive tasks. An adjustable bench can be set higher for weaving and lower for threading. Instead of bending over, work at eye level. You can partly fold some

Weave Your Project

Mini-Runner #1: Weave with the same yarn as the warp for 32"; this includes 2" for each hem, plus 28" for the runner. Cut from the loom and slip knot the warp over-edge to secure ends. Wet-finish as I indicate later in this chapter. Hem ends.

Mini-Runner #2: Weave an inch of plain weave; put in two cardboard spacers 2" wide in each plain weave shed. Weave 3 picks, then hemstitch across as in Chapter 4 (see page 66). A magnifying lamp is a great help here. After 1", switch to the second color. Weave 26" light, 1" dark as before; hemstitch with dark; put in two spacers 2" wide, weave 1". Cut off, remove the spacers and secure the edges of the fringe plain weaves. After wet-finishing, cut off evenly across for fringe.

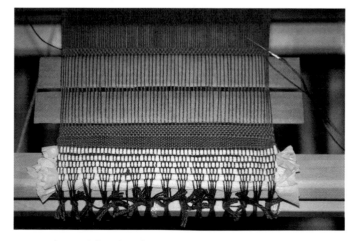

Weave three picks, then hemstitch across.

Start a New Yarn: Both mini-runners begin and end with the same color yarn as in the warp. When you run out of yarn on your bobbin or change color as for Mini-Runner #2, you need to start a new yarn. Let a few inches of the previous yarn hang out the side. Change the shed. Place that yarn in this next shed over 3-4 warps, tug it down between the warps, under and toward you. Throw the new yarn in the same shed, also letting a few inches of yarn hang out the side. Because old and new yarns overlap by

TIP

To reduce bulk, use a lighter-weight weft yarn for just the hem areas.

a few warps, they lock together. After wet-finishing, cut these ends right to the cloth. They are essentially invisible. For rayon, silk, and other slippery yarns, overlap a bit more.

Always cut each yarn—never break it. Breaking the yarn stretches and weakens it. If, however, you decide to change a yarn in the middle of the weaving and not at the edges, like with heavy rug yarns, you can break the threads to overlap them in the shed, making the change more invisible. You can also fray the ends, open up the ply, and insert one into the other.

Tension problems? If all threads on the loom are not evenly tensioned across, the shed can be uneven, and your shuttle will catch on threads below. Tension problems can result in uneven beating as well as other serious weaving problems. Edges are especially prone to stretching; shown here is a method I use to add weight to soft edges, as well as to correct other tension problems when they occur. I buy aluminum chain link in groups of three, four, six, etc. Tie a thread around the chain and around the threads in question. Some threads require more weighting than others to do the job (the more links, the more weight). If whole groups become loose across, a bar with holes in the ends can be put to work with the chain links tied to the holes, the bar put through the problem threads, and hung over the back beam.

Aluminum chain links tied around selvedge threads.

Weavers around the World

In other cultures, such as Slovakia in Central Europe, women weave on horizontal floor looms.

Margita from Hel'pa weaves a variety of home textiles including clothing, tablecloths, and rugs. She creates very complex and incredibly beautiful patterned cloth of cotton and wool using just a stick to pick up the patterns. She saves these patterns with more sticks at the back of the loom. She wove gorgeous shirts for her three sons' weddings.

Photo by Sigrid Piroch.

Broken thread? If you break a warp, it may occur at the edge where there is extra wear, but it can occur anywhere across. Tie a new thread several yards in length to the broken thread at the front; slip them through the reed and heddle to the back. With the new thread in the reed and heddle, cut off the broken thread and let it hang over the back beam. In the front, tie the new thread around a pin in the woven cloth as a figure 8 and dip the end of the pin into the cloth to hold it. At the back, weight it, perhaps with a single chain link. Weave for a few inches. Tie the broken thread to the new thread at the back; pull through the heddle and reed. Tie it into the cloth as a figure 8 and cut out the substitute thread. When the cloth is off the loom, with a large blunt-eye needle, run these threads back into the weaving, overlapping them in the warp direction as they would have been woven. After wet-finishing, trim close for an almost invisible solution.

Put in a Cutting Line: When weaving a set of items such as napkins, a cutting line makes it easy to cut them apart later and helps straighten the warp and even out the tension, similar to spreading the warp at the beginning of the warp. Throw a contrasting yarn in a plain weave shed. Don't beat, but change to the other shed and throw another pick. Repeat without beating several times and then gently work the weft yarns back with the beater as far as possible. Switch to your regular weft and continue.

Weaving mistakes? If you notice an error right away you can unweave—reverse the weaving—in process. If you've woven more than a few inches, sometimes it is possible to carefully cut between warp threads and slip out the weft. (If threads are very fragile, they might not stand up to weaving, unweaving, and weaving again.) You can also correct later off-loom.

Extra warp? With extra warp, experiment with different treadlings and yarns of different weights, fibers, and/or colors. If there is considerable warp

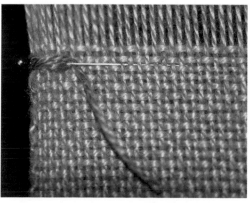

The replacement thread is tied in a figure 8 around a pin.

left on the loom, you might be able to weave another project. You can also save it for another day by securing the weaver's cross: from the front, open each plain weave shed and place a lease stick into each shed. Tie the ends with a slip knot in front of the sticks to secure the warp, then chain off. This can be used as a sample or project warp, or if long enough, tied onto another warp.

Cut the Weaving from the Loom: Since you're near the end of the warp, first tape the rod down so when you cut, the rod doesn't pull the warp through the reed and heddles. Cut the fabric off, using the front beam as a guide so the warp is cut evenly. Tie the warp in bundles in front of the reed; should you decide to make another warp of the same sett and threading, you can tie onto it. Secure fabric ends with a zigzag sewing machine stitch, a serger, or overcast by hand.

Correct Errors Before Wet-Finishing: Hold your runner up to a good light to check for errors. Correct them with a needle using extra warp/weft. Clip any skips in the fabric and run the substitute thread in and out as it should have been woven, beginning and ending with just a few threads overlapping at each end. After wet-finishing, clip these right to the fabric. Holding the fabric up to the light will also help you see how evenly you beat.

Wet-Finish Your Runner: Soak in warm water with neutral soap. Lay flat to avoid wrinkling. Rinse well, again without wrinkling, and roll up in a towel to pull out moisture. Snap to block, hang to dry, and steam press when almost dry. If you hemstitched, trim off the plain weave at each end—your fringe will be freshly cut and look brand new.

Storage: If you store handwovens for any period of time, wrap them around an acid-free tube or one lined with acid-free paper. Watch for critters.

What's next? Make another warp and weave again soon so you get into a rhythm for each task. With practice, your hands will remember the movements even when your mind is busy planning more weavings. Front-to-back warping is one of three basic methods of warping. Depending on your equipment, circumstances, experience, and the types of weaving you do, you will probably develop variations that suit your style. A change at any point will affect the whole process. Be open to new ideas, but don't compromise quality. Every warp has at least one surprise from which to learn. That's what makes it fun and so wonderfully *magical.*

Smile, You're Weaving

Laura Fry, a Canadian Master Weaver and production weaver from Prince George, British Columbia, wove this lovely afghan in 2/2 twill of singles wool in royal blue, magenta, and burgundy.

Photo by Joe Coca.

Handwoven fabric is especially sumptuous when made of wool and silk. This project is simple for you to work in plain weave, the same structure as the last project, but in a luxury yarn. The silk adds extra sparkle and the wool adds softness. This time there is more than one color in the warp (a plaid scarf woven with stripe emphasis) together with a few new lessons. Although planned for a table loom, this can be woven on any loom. By weaving this project, you are keeping your promise to make a warp, dress a loom, and weave again soon. Smile, you're weaving!

Lindsey Pirson in her plaid spring coat, scarf, and tam made from Sigrid Piroch's woven fabric.

Meet Lindsey Pirson, age 3, wearing her new plaid spring coat, scarf, and tam. After I wove the fabric, Lindsey's grandmother, Evelyn Pirson, sewed it for her.

To weave this asymmetrical plaid perfectly balanced (same number of warp and weft threads per inch after wet-finishing), the beat needs to be

Stronger vertical stripes make for a more flattering cloth.

precise and even throughout. Plaid squares require more yardage to match for sewing; asymmetricals require even more yardage and are even trickier to match. I sett this project a little closer in the warp, visually changing this plaid to stronger vertical stripes that alternate with subtle color-blending stripes.

The drafts show two-color repeats with three warp and weft colors. The two-shaft version has been expanded to four shafts using straight twill; treadling is still just two treadles, but now each is tied up to two shafts. Note the horizontal and vertical *color bars* in the drafts, representing the color of each warp and each weft thread. There are 18 threads in one color repeat, with two color repeats in these drafts, yet one structure repeat is only two threads in each direction.

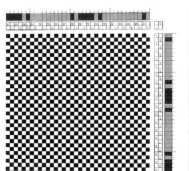

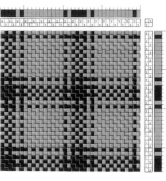

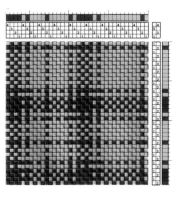

This plain weave fabric can be woven on two shafts (as in the structural draft and the color-and-weave effect draft), but this time you have graduated to four shafts. Both produce the exact same fabric, but on four there is less friction on threads and more treadling choices if you wish to use them.

Child's or Adult's Scarf in Plain Weave Tri-Color Silk-Wool and Child's Tam

Select and Plan Your Project: Decide to weave the child's scarf, child's scarf and tam, or adult's scarf. The child's scarf is 36" long on the loom, the adult's scarf is 45"; both are 9" wide in the reed, hemmed (no fringe).

Determine the Number of Warp Threads: One color repeat is 18 threads; for a scarf 9" wide at 24 epi, make a warp of 12 color repeats equalling 216 threads; begin and end with 4 red threads, so add 4 to balance equalling 220 threads total.

Determine Warp Length: Start with the length of the item(s) to be woven. Adjust for expected shrinkage plus take-up, loom waste, and sampling. (If you weave these projects on a floor loom, add another half yard for additional loom waste.)

Child's Scarf: Plan a ½ yard for loom waste on a table loom and another ½ yard for a 12" sample to check threads and sett, wet-finish, and tie on again equalling 1 yard total. Sampling tells us that take-up and shrinkage for these threads is in the range of 10 percent, so for a 36" finished child's scarf, you need to weave approximately 40", just over 1 yard. Allow 2½ yards total warp.

Adult's Scarf: Add ½ yard more, 3 yards total.

Tam: For a matching child's tam, check pattern pieces, taking into account matching stripes as well as piecing for any pattern pieces wider than 9". This totals 1½ yards of fabric, including take-up and shrinkage.

Child's Scarf and Tam: 2½ yards plus 1½ yards equals 4 yards total.

PROJECT LAYOUT:

Project	Child's or Adult's Scarf and Child's Tam
Equipment	2- or 4-shaft loom and 3 shuttles
Structure	Plain Weave
Threads and Colors	3 colors JaggerSpun 18/2 silk-wool at 5,040 yd./lb. for warp and weft—50 percent fine Tussah silk and 50 percent Merino wool, mothproofed. Two colors can be similar and mid-value, but not necessarily the same color family; the third color can either be very light or very dark. (This project uses medium pink and medium gray for the mid-values and dark red.)
Sett	24 epi, double in a 12 dpi reed
Width in Reed	9"
Make a Warp	220 x 2½ yards for child's scarf = 550 yards, 220 x 4 = 880 yards for child's scarf and tam, or 220 x 3 = 660 yards for adult's scarf. These include 12 color repeats plus 4 red threads to balance.
Estimate Weft	Since this project is slightly warp-faced, you will use slightly less weft than warp.

Make a Warp: For the child's scarf and tam, make it 4 yards long of 220 threads. Change colors as indicated in the color bar of the draft by cutting the end of one color and tying on the next with an overhand knot, but only at the first or last peg. Begin on the warping board with 4 red threads (down and up twice). Cut that thread at the top and tie on one gray thread, which is then cut at the bottom, then wind 1 red thread, which is cut at the top; continue on with four gray, one pink, one gray, four pink, one red, one pink and repeat. The full warp is made with 12 color repeats plus four reds; that is, it begins and ends with four red threads. (If you want to double the selvedge threads, you will need one extra thread each side—treat the doubled thread as one.)

Thread the Loom: To keep track of the color order, begin each color repeat by moving over 18 heddles on their respective shafts, one color repeat, and 18 threads in the lease sticks. When you have threaded 18 warps, you should have used all 18 heddles.

Shuttle Rotation: Use three shuttles. Fill three bobbins, one of each color. When you throw/catch a shuttle, put it down horizontally at that side in front of any other shuttle(s); pick up another shuttle, either side, and throw/catch it as before, placing it in front of any previous shuttle. Do this even when colors are used out of sequence. This method assures that threads wrap around each other consistently at the edges. The new thread should always cross *over* the

Weave your sample in the same color order as you warped. Though colors and shuttles change order, treadling always alternates treadle 1 and treadle 2, which on a table loom means lifting 1-3 and then 2-4. Use all three colors for an asymmetrical plaid (left side) or any one color at a time for warp stripes (right side). Weave a sample to find the most effective; usually the darkest color looks best. Weave the scarf 40".

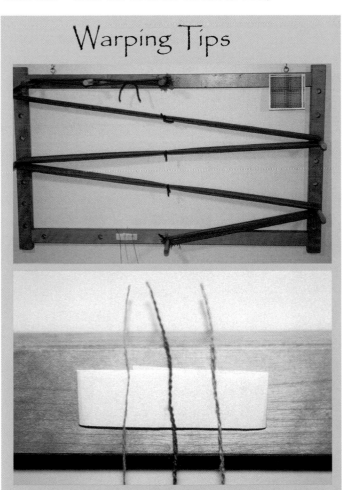

Warping Tips

1. Mount the color draft on or near the warping board so you can keep track of the color sequence.
2. A piece of masking tape or Velcro™ on the warping board holds thread ends for quick color changes.
3. To make handling finer threads easier, moisten your fingers.
4. Try this exercise: lightly move your thumb across your fingertips, then across the palm of your hand, which is more sensitive. Warping with just the ends of your fingers does not give as much feedback about the threads as allowing the threads to also slip through your palms. This gives sensitive feedback, making it easier to use finer threads and to feel knots to cut out.

Shuttles prepared for rotation.

previous thread as it enters the shed. If this does not happen with the standard sequence above, work out a sequence that does.

Change Colors: In a sample, you do not need to cut the colors as you try various combinations. As you weave this project, you do not need to cut the thread each time you change a color because it does not travel far before being used again.

If you don't use a color soon, cut that thread and start a new thread. If this happens frequently, especially with heavy threads, sides build up a "smile" so you no longer have a flat web to beat against. To minimize this, start one thread from the right and the next from the left.

Finish: Cut, overedge, wet-finish with warm-to-cool water, steam press when almost dry, and hem. This slightly warp-faced sett in the reed is 24 epi; the finished fabric has 18 ppi.

Other Project Ideas

1. For a perfectly squared plaid, as shown in the drawdown, sett the warp a little wider for a balanced 50/50 weave. As sett varies with width in the reed, determine sett by sampling.

2. This project is sett at 24 epi, evenly dented double in a 12 reed or equivalent (see *Sett Chart* on page 43). Consider uneven denting to add more texture and interest in the cloth. For example, sley 2/2/3 across in a 10 reed for 25 epi.

3. Substitute 18/2 or 20/2 worsted wool at the same sett for a slightly heartier scarf. If you substitute a heavier wool thread, it will weave up faster and will produce a heavier fabric.

4. You can, of course, make a wider and longer warp on a wider loom for coat yardage. Select a pattern and determine how wide the cloth will need to

Additional Fabrics: The same plaid design in wool is woven with a different color plan—2 medium and 1 light blue in warp and weft.

A 4-shaft huck lace is woven with sewing thread at 44 epi for lining fabric to match the coat.

be at the pattern's widest point, with or without piecing. Since the wider the warp, the more resistance to beating in the weft, what weaves at 18 epi at 9" wide for this project is likely to sett at 15 epi (or less) on a wider warp. Take into account draw-in and remember that often handwovens can be planned with minimal seams, or by using selvedges as finished edges.

Pointers on Wear, Abrasion, and Breakage:
Although I had no breakage weaving this warp, as threads become finer, weavers often worry more about breakage. Fine threads may have little strength individually, but working together in a warp, they may be quite strong. Here are some tips:

- Use two or more medium to fine threads in each dent.
- Beating on a closed shed is harder on edges than on an open shed.
- If some threads are weaker, place them on the front shafts where there is less stress, adjusting the draft.
- Move your warp often, every inch or less.

- Threads may untwist at cut ends and be weaker at the start of the warp; expect less breakage as you weave further into the warp.
- No one throws a shuttle exactly the same from each side. Evaluate how yours differs and any effect it has on the woven cloth.
- Check that warp threads are all advancing exactly straight from the back beam to the front.
- If one edge of the warp wears or breaks more, move the reed a fraction of an inch in that direction.
- If the same threads break more than once, check to see if your reed is rusty or heddle eye is sharp; some types of heddles are easier on threads than others.
- Fuzz balls or a broken thread can tangle a warp and cause more breakage.
- Watch for fraying at the edges and stress leading to breakage. Try using a temple.
- Rolling on a warp with a raddle (back to front warping) is easier on threads than rolling them through the heddles twice (front to back warping).

Specialty Art Weavings

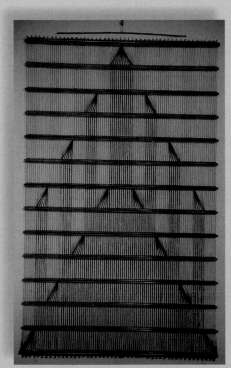

Peter Collingwood of Colchester, England is certainly one of the most influential weavers of our time. His classic books on rugs, cardweaving, sprang, and split-ply braiding come out of a lifetime of research with a major impact on weavers of our generation. Here are two of his weavings.

Macrogauze "M 227" of black, natural and bleached linen with rods, 52" x 33".

Macrogauze "M 226" of natural and black linen with steel rods, 56" x 36".

9 Weave a Rainbow

Two Maya women, wearing their huipils from Zunil, Guatemala, hold a backstrap loom with a brocaded skirt in the process of being woven.

Photo by Gianni Vecchiato.

The projects in this chapter illustrate how to warp a floor loom *back to front,* the second classic warping method. The first projects in this book were warped *front to back* on a table loom, but could have been warped by this second method.

Since this method can also be used on a table loom, this project can be woven on a table loom if it has a wide enough weaving width and enough shafts. A table loom uses levers while a floor loom uses treadles (which you'll learn to tie up in this chapter).

Color Gamps. Color is a very different experience in fiber than in any other art medium. For example, a painter creates using pigment while a stained glass worker creates using light. In fiber, both happen at once.

Color Gamps: Many weavers are uncomfortable designing with color, so weaving a color gamp is an excellent way to view colors in action and it is an excellent color reference for future projects. A "color gamp" or "color blanket" is threaded with sections of color across, then each section is woven with these same colors. As each color block develops, it crosses with itself as it mixes with each of the others.

Munsell® Color-Order System: This color gamp project uses the Munsell Color-Order System with its five principle hues: red, yellow, green, blue, and purple. Professor Albert H. Munsell first published his system in 1905, establishing numerical scales with visually uniform steps for the qualities of color. Today, the Munsell System is an international color and science standard used by companies as diverse as archaeological institutes, Evan Picone, and Hershey.

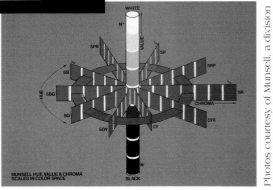

The Munsell 3-D Color Tree (above) and the Munsell Color Space cutaway (right).

At the turn of the last century, color was not well understood. Many different color theories were advanced, but none could be confirmed until later, after the physics of color became understood. There was the Newton system with seven primaries (yellow, green, blue, indigo, violet, red, and orange); Ives with three (magenta, yellow, and turquoise blue); Otswald with four primaries (yellow, red, ultramarine blue, and sea green), but with 24 hues in-between; Berga with 40 sectors divided into four (yellow, red, blue, and green); and the Hiler Color Circle with 30 primaries. Although not as accurate as mixing primaries, it is the Goethe-Brewster color wheel with its three primaries that has won over the population worldwide, perhaps because of its simplicity.

Any color system must deal with the three physical characteristics of color: hue, value, and chroma. A century later, with new challenges, the use of color is changing again. A computer monitor uses light and a printer uses pigment, requiring new approaches to color. In fact, there is a veritable war among supporters of various color systems for the computer, not to mention various Internet, scientific, and brand names. There are and will continue to be many new ways to read color as we reshape our color environment over the next century.

Color Gamps

The Munsell models show, in their natural order, the placement of all possible colors according to the three attributes of color: hue, value, and chroma. These show the logical progression of *equal* color steps where every possible color has a home. Each color is placed *visually* where it belongs, seen in its logical relationship to every other color, and codified using the decimal system. Weavers work with colors visually, so this is an ideal color system to use for color and design planning. Note that by placing each hue (color) in relation to its chroma (intensity) and value (light to dark), models are lopsided.

In the Color Tree, the lightest and brightest pure hue is yellow bulging out atop; the darkest here at maximum intensity is violet, which falls at a much lower value. This system is an intriguing way to approach color; one immediately applicable to fibers.

Inspired by the Munsell Color-Order System, this project warps with 10/2 cotton yarns in 20 colors: five primaries and three interim colors. Weave with these same 20 *colors* (chromatics) with seven additional *yarns*, white to black through gray, that are *without color* (achromatics). Weave one or all of the four color gamps in the four structures listed below:

PROJECT LAYOUT:

Gamp	Structure	Equipment Minimum
Gamp One	Plain Weave	2-shaft loom
Gamp Two	Herringbone 2/2 Twill and Reverse	4-shaft loom
Gamp Three	Two Block 3/1-1/3 Twill	8-shaft loom
Gamp Four	Brighton Honeycomb	8-shaft loom
Yarns	10/2 mercerized cotton for warp and weft at 4200 yd./lb. in Lunatic Fringe's 20 colors + 7 neutral 10/2s for weft (white to black through grays). NOTE: this project can also be woven at the same setts with 18/2 wool at 5040 yd./lb. or 20/2 wool at 5600 yd./lb.	
Sett	24 epi for Gamps One and Two, double in a 12 reed; 30 epi for Gamps Three and Four, double in a 15 reed (or 2/3 across in a 12)	
Width in Reed	25" for Gamps One and Two; 20" wide for Gamps Three and Four	
Make Warp and Figure Weft	For all four gamps: 600 threads (30 each color x 20 colors) + double-edge threads + one extra thread each side for floating selvedges = 604 threads x 6 yards long = 3624 yards total warp; multiply by 2 for total warp and weft – 7248; divide by 20 colors for yardage for each color = approximately 360 yards.	

NOTE: If you plan to weave all four gamps, begin with Gamp Three and/or Four first because the sett for them is closer: 30 epi. Next weave the other two gamps, Gamp One and/or Two, by cutting off and re-denting the threads in the reed at 24 epi.

Warping the Loom Back to Front

This chapter introduces warping back to front, step-by-step. If you have an 8-shaft loom, you can weave all four gamps with a 6-yard warp. If you have a 4-shaft loom, you can weave Gamps One and Two with four yards. If you have a 2-shaft loom, you can weave Gamp One with only two yards. All other information is the same for each, including the number of colors and threads.

Begin as before when warping front to back, by first making the warp. If using a warping board, make two chains since it is unlikely all the threads will fit on the pegs: wind half the warp and chain off, then the other half and chain again. Tie and insert the lease sticks in the weaver's cross;

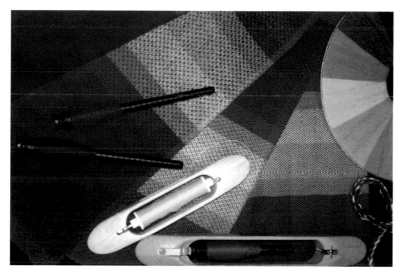

anchor these lease sticks loosely on the front beam using masking tape or painter's tape at each end, all as before. Remove the reed from the beater (see photo above).

Cut the ties holding the cross, ease open the threads, and space apart. Pull out about a foot of each of the 20 color bundles (that is, each group of 30 threads), cut the end of each of the warp loops, and tie each color group around a stick. Use the same knot used to tie the warp to rods.

WEAVERS AROUND THE WORLD

In southeast Asia, textiles are woven with incredibly fine silk threads to create intricate and lustrous patterns.

Khamla Phomalune is skillfully weaving a discontinuous supplementary weft patterning at Carol Cassidy's Lao Textiles in Vientiane, Laos ... and wearing it, too! An ingenious vertical storage device called a Khao Yai is made up of clasped heddle strings into which sticks are inserted to save as many as 1000 weft patterns. Handwoven clothing of cotton and silk is worn every day.

Some weavers do not cut the warp, but instead place the uncut threads around a stick or bar and proceed. Some weavers make their cross at the end so they do not have to cut or move the lease sticks later in the process. Cutting and tying assures me these warp threads will not slip when rolled on or when woven off. All methods are legitimate. Try them all, then decide.

If this stick is the same size as the space in the beater where the reed sits, put the stick into this space while working to secure the threads. The warp has been spaced, bundled, cut, and tied around the stick in the reed slot.

Move the lease sticks behind the heddles. If you add screw eyes on each side of the back of the castle an inch above the eye of the heddles, you can attach lease sticks with a strong thread.

Pull out the warp and space it across in the **raddle**. This raddle, with one-inch segments, mounts on this loom on the back beam. Move the lease sticks to the back of the loom, the warp spaced at one-inch intervals across in the raddle. The sett for the first gamps (Three and Four) is 30 epi, so each raddle section holds one color group of 30 threads.

The lease sticks moved to the back of the loom. The top is placed on the raddle, and the warp is ready to wind on.

System Texsolv is shown securing the lease sticks together and attaching them to a screw eye.

The top is placed on the raddle, the warp ready to wind on. Roll on the warp.

Pirns are wound with cottons, 20 in colors and seven in white to black through grays. Since only one color is woven at a time, you need only one shuttle and you can use fewer bobbins or pirns by loading any one with the current color. It is most important that yarns be properly wound and edges taut to work against.

Weaving with Bobbins and End-Delivery Shuttles: The last projects used a boat shuttle with a bobbin. This project uses an end-delivery shuttle with a pirn. You can use either shuttle type for any project in this book that uses yarns. For finer threads and more perfect selvedges, an end-delivery shuttle is recommended.

Some shuttles use a bobbin that rotates; the yarn unwinds from a hole in the center of the side. There is no mechanism to control tension. To stop the bobbin, use your third or fourth finger from underneath or your thumb from on top. It is important for the thread to catch properly at the edge. Use a bobbin-shuttle for loft in a weaving.

An end-delivery shuttle uses a pirn that does not rotate; the thread is pulled off the end through a tensioner and exits through an eye at the end of the shuttle. The thread automatically stops and catches the edge with the same tension each time, so the weaver need not be concerned about either. The shuttle tension should be adjusted for the type of yarn and result intended. *(End-delivery shuttles with metal tips are mill shuttles and are used by handweavers only if they use it with equipment called a fly shuttle box mounted on the beater. A fly shuttle can be seen in the countermarch loom photos.)*

If you wish to use an end-delivery shuttle, you will want to practice filling a pirn. Loop the beginning thread over so it catches as the pirn first turns, just as with a bobbin. With an electric bobbin winder, you can use two hands for light tension on the thread. Fill a pirn from the large end with a quick sideways zigzag motion over about an inch, gradually moving across left so the threads are always taken up at a slight angle. Consequently, a thread can never slip down into a previous row and will release evenly when the shuttle is thrown. (The white pirn in the photo shows the shape of the pirn when filled.)

Pirns wound with cottons.

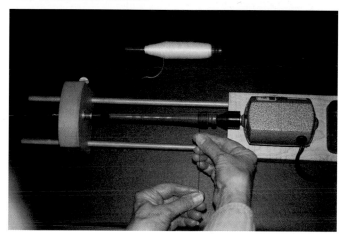

Filling a pirn.

Drawdowns: *Always* do a structural drawdown before you warp and weave. If the project is in color, do a color-and-weave effect drawdown as well. Many weaving books contain errors, so always check.

Thread the loom according to the draft selected, depending on which gamp(s) you will weave. The drafts are as follows:

1. Gamp One: Thread the loom for plain weave on 2 shafts alternating 1 and 2 in the threading and treadling.
2. Gamp Two: Thread the loom for twill on 4 shafts and treadle 2/2 herringbone twill treadling 1 to 4 and repeat, then reverse; you can also weave the plain-weave gamp.
3. Gamp Three can include all four gamps. Thread twill 1 to 8 and repeat.

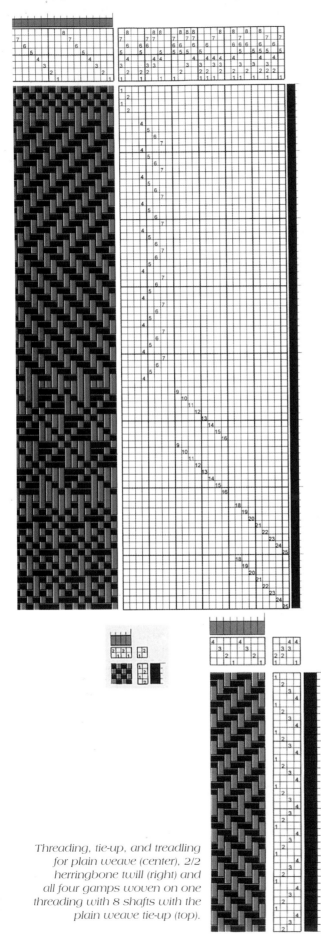

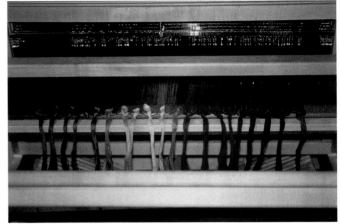

Remove the raddle after the warp is rolled on. Thread the heddles from the lease sticks, then remove the lease sticks.

The reed is dented across, centering the threads.

Tie the threads on the front bar using the same tie as on the back. Except with plain weave, use a floating selvedge on each side.

Threading, tie-up, and treadling for plain weave (center), 2/2 herringbone twill (right) and all four gamps woven on one threading with 8 shafts with the plain weave tie-up (top).

Drafts: Drafts show two repeats of warp for each. Note that it takes 22 treadle tie-ups to weave all these in the illustrations. If you have a 22-treadle loom (or a computer-assist), you can proceed. To weave with an 8-shaft loom, you will need to tie-up for one, weave, and re-tie for the next. Don't cut off the warp— just re-tie the treadles. The most you will need at any one time is 8 treadles, and since most 8-shaft looms have

10 treadles, you can also tie-up plain weave for headings.

Weave all 20 warp colors in the same order as the threading for each sampler for a plaid, following the draft. The four color gamps (plain weave, 2/2 herringbone twill, 2 blocks 3/1 twill, and Brighton honeycomb) are each woven with the same number of picks of each color weft as there are warp threads in that color (30). The exception is 2/2 herringbone twill that weaves 30 picks forward, and because it reverses and does not repeat, 29 picks back. Next, weave 30 picks with each of the seven neutrals from white to black.

Weaving Twill: Watch the twill line as it develops. It should be straight, not wavering. With a lighter beat, the twill line will move up at a more vertical angle; that also happens if your sett is closer. With a harder beat, the twill line will slant more horizontally, which also happens if you open up the sett more. Once off the loom, hold the fabric up to the light to check for consistency of beat.

Finish by soaking the gamps in a tub of very warm water with neutral soap. Rinse thoroughly, roll up in a towel, block and hang to dry, and steam press when almost dry.

Some Design Thoughts: Color gamps give you the opportunity to observe the interaction of the colors. The top wrapping shows how you can warp using 20 colors, each one wrapped 30 times as in this project. The bottom wrapping shows how you can blend these 20 colors to get 39. This is accomplished by using the pure color for 15 strands, then alternating this color with the next color for 15, then the next pure color for 15, and repeat across.

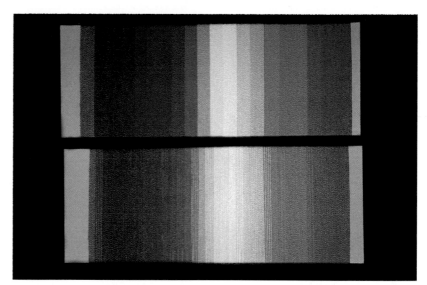

The top wrapping shows a warp using 20 colors and the bottom wrapping blends the same colors to get 39.

Color wheel and gamps in wool.

Wool Color Gamp

If you wish to make a color gamp with fewer colors, here is one of wool made up of only three primaries plus the secondaries (on the previous page). Note how a darker weft enriches the colors it crosses, whereas lighter threads white-out these same colors. Gather up yarns on-hand to see if you have enough. This project uses 2/7 Klippans/Ullgarn, a Swedish wool, for warp and weft.

Warp: Thread 12 colors across the warp, 2" per color equals 24". (24" warp x 12 epi = 288 threads total.)

Weft: Use the same colors and color order, plus black/white/gray if available; sett is 12 epi and 12 ppi after finishing for a 50/50 weave.

You can dye colors over white using any color model and any series of fibers. For three primaries, dye the pure colors and then mix an equal amount of each set of two for the secondaries. For Munsell, to produce 20 colors, begin with the five pure colors and then mix each set of the five interim colors with its neighbor, and then once again.

Color Wheel: Cut a circle out of cardboard and cut out a smaller circle in the center. Wrap the yarns around, taping ends on the back; threads overlapping at the center.

Which Warping Method to Use: Front-to-back or back-to-front? Although there is no one "right way," there are advantages and disadvantages for each method. Most projects can be done either way, but different equipment and projects point the way to different approaches. Be flexible so you can pick the one most appropriate for you and your equipment.

Warping Front to Back

Get off to a fast start denting and threading.

There's no need for a raddle.

The chained warp may be in the way while denting and threading if working from the front; in addition, if it sits for a while, it may be subject to abrasion.

Lease sticks, which keep the weaver's cross, do not need to be moved at any point in the process.

You can add threads to warp chains if needed before the warp is rolled on.

Because warp is threaded through reed and heddles before rolling on, it is put through more wear and tear, especially important with fine or fragile threads.

Some *looms* are easier to dent and thread from the front—this depends partly on whether you can see and reach the heddles, and whether or not parts of the loom can be taken off to reach inside.

Some *warps* are easier to dent and/or thread from the front, such as unevenly dented warps, warps with many different threads and/or colors, and complex combinations of denting and threading.

Since lease sticks can be removed after denting and threading, but before rolling on, there may be less stress on each thread. But once they are removed, they cannot help even tension across.

Threads must be cut at the beginning of warping to dent and thread, so you must tie on at the back as well as the front.

Warping Back to Front

Get off to a fast start rolling on the warp.

A raddle is needed.

The chained warp is out of the way for threading and denting.

At some point in the process, with some methods, the lease sticks that keep the weaver's cross will need to be moved behind the heddles in order to thread them. In others it is anchored there at the beginning with the raddle on the back beam.

After the warp is rolled on, you can't add threads to the warp chain, so any threads added later may have to be weighted and hung over the back beam. Extra threads, however, can be planned "just in case."

Since the warp is threaded through the heddles and reed after rolling on, it is easier on a fine or fragile warp.

Some *looms* are easier to thread and dent from the back.

Some *warps* are easier to thread and/or dent from the back.

Since the lease sticks are not removed before rolling on, there may be more stress on each thread, but this may help keep the tension even.

In one method, uncut threads are put around a rod before rolling on—saving time tying on at the back. However, if later you tie a warp onto this warp, not being anchored, some threads may tend to slip around the rod.

Hint

If you thread from the back of the loom, you can turn the threading draft upside down so the draft matches the shaft order.

Fabulous Installations

Photo by Dieter Beck.

Ulrike Beck is a Master Weaver from Germany now living in Harlem, Georgia. Her weavings are of linen warp with wefts of assorted fibers like cotton, wool, and mixtures. "Dual Prismatic, 36" x 170", woven on a fine linen warp.

Peter Collingwood's 3D macrogauze in reds of linen with steel rods, 25 feet high and 40 inches square; this hangs in a stairwell at 400 Unicorn Park, Woburn, Boston, Massachusetts.

10 Vested Interests

Sigrid Piroch's high fashion 24-shaft "Break Vest" of silks in greens and black. (Sewn by Carol McGuire of Clarion, Pennsylvania; modeled by Christen Piroch)

Weave a color-and-weave effect sampler for a library of patterns. On a 4-shaft twill threading, with just three structures and four colors, you can create a sampler of hundreds of colorful patterns. Chances are, you will still be using this for reference many years from now.

This sampler is threaded as straight twill on 4 shafts; each of nine sections is a different color sequence. Each is treadled in the same color order, first plain weave, then 3/1 twill, and finally Rosepath. You are familiar with 3/1 twill because this is the structure for jeans.

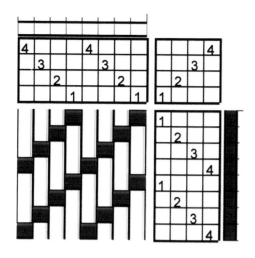

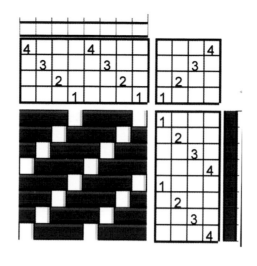

This reversible weave skips over 1 thread and under 3 in both warp and weft.

To draft, thread, and weave twills, plus twill relatives like overshot, it is necessary to understand **twill order**. In twill order, the threading and treadling always move one thread/number forward or back, odd-to-even or even-to-odd (for example, 3 to 4 or 2 to 1). These never skip from odd-to-odd (for example, to 1).

1 to 3) or even to even (2 to 4). Many people have difficulty visualizing twills because threads on the first and last shafts of a draft (for example, 1 and 4 or 1 and 8) don't logically seem to continue on the diagonal. Nor do they on a loom where 8 is at the back of the loom and 1 is at the front.

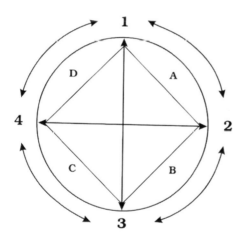

Circle drafting on 1-4 shafts.

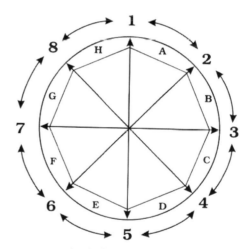

Circle drafting on 1-8 shafts.

Circle Drafting

Circle drafting makes it easy to figure out how to stay in twill order—just follow the arrows in either direction around the circle, never skipping across. Circle drafting is shown on 1 to 4 shafts (or A to D blocks) and 1 to 8 shafts (or A to H blocks).

Twill threaded as "straight draw" is threaded 1, 2, straight through to X (the last shaft). Its many different patterns are created just by using diagonal tie-ups.

Rosepath is used here as the *treadling* for one section of the sampler. Point twill, a close relative, can

be threaded 1-2-3-4-3-2 and repeat, the threading on the draft looking every bit like a point. Adding one thread creates Rosepath, one of the most popular threadings of all time: 1-2-3-4-1-4-3-2 and repeat. Variations include the following three:

    1-2-3-4-1-4-3-2-1-4
    4-3-2-1-4-1-2-3
    4-3-2-1-4-1-2-3-4-1

Color-and-Weave Effect Sampler

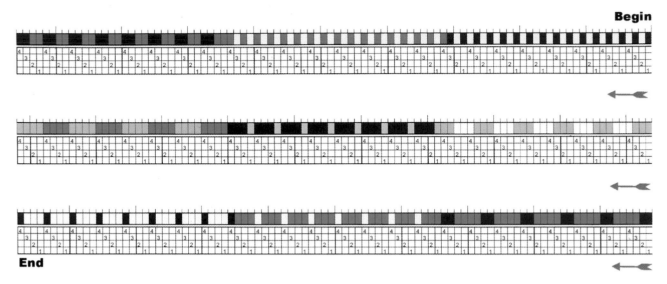

Begin

End

It's project time! To create a color-and-weave effect sampler, make the warp according to the color order in the draft. Read the color bars with the numbers, right to left for each line of the draft. This design is built around nine color blocks of approximately 32 threads each, adjusted so the color sequences fit together. Since it begins and ends with blue, use a blue floating selvedge on each side and a doubled blue edge thread.

Block 1 is 1 blue and 1 white alternating and ending blue (31 threads)

Block 2 is 1 green and 1 white ending green (32)

Block 3 is 2 green and 2 blue ending blue (33)

Block 4 is 3 gold and 3 white ending gold (33)

Block 5 is 3 blue and 1 gold ending blue (31)

Block 6 is 4 green and 4 gold ending gold (32)

Block 7 is 2 blue and 4 green ending blue (32)

Block 8 is 3 green and 1 white ending green (31)

Block 9 is 1 blue and 3 white ending blue (33)

Sampler warp threads: 288 plus 1 floating selvedge each side plus 1 doubled thread each side equals 292 total.

Before tying on to the ends of the color gamp from the previous chapter, re-dent and center the previous warp in an 8-dent reed at the new sett (from double in a 15 reed to double in an 8-dent reed). Proceed with the "front to back" warping method. This tie-on method saves rethreading heddles. (Or, of course, you can warp from scratch.)

Tip

Lift the knots to the center of the reed to help them pass through more easily. (If knots with another yarn do not fit through the reed or the heddle eyes, a flatter knot is needed, so use a square knot.)

PROJECT LAYOUT:

Project	Weave a sampler from which the vest weaving pattern is selected
Equipment	2-shaft or 4-shaft loom, plus 2 shuttles
Structure	2 shafts for plain weave, 4 shafts for 2/2 twill and rosepath
Yarns/Colors	Warp and weft is 5/2 mercerized cotton at 2100 yd./lb.; colors from Halcyon Yarn—Gold #11, White #105, Green #136 and Navy #132; vest is Navy and Gold.
Sett	16 epi, 2 per dent in an 8 dpi reed
Width in Reed	Approximately 18⅛"
Make Warps	(1) Sampler: 292 threads x 4 yards = 1168 yards for 4 colors = 164 yards Gold, 308 yards White, 324 yards Navy, 372 yards Green; (2) Vest: 292 threads x 4 yards = 1168 yards for 2 colors = 584 yards each color
Estimate weft	For this balanced twill, the weft yardage for each color is the same yardage as the warp yardage

The first color segment is tied to the previous warp (above and upper right), then all across (lower right).

The overhand knot, or circle knot, is used here to tie the new warp on to the previous warp, one thread at a time. Twist the two threads together to the right (clockwise), ending with the ends coming through from the back.

Two repeats of threading. Treadling draft, top to bottom, shows two repeats of each structure with a space between each: (1) treadling for plain weave is treadle 5-6 and repeat; (2) twill treadle 1-2-3-4 and repeat; (3) treadle 4-3-2-1 and repeat for reverse twill; and (4) treadle 1-2-3-4-1-4-3-2 and repeat for Rosepath.

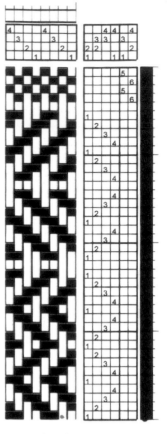

Weave Your Project

Follow the threading color order for each of these weaves: plain weave, 3/1 twill, 3/1 twill reversed, and Rosepath. For example, the first color block is blue and white alternating for 31 picks. Take the threading color bar and turn it sideways for the treadling color bar. Now weave the entire sequence of colors with the plain weave treadling, then repeat the full color bar with the twill treadling forward and then back again.

Finally, repeat it again for Rosepath. If you have extra warp at the end, experiment—try treadling some of the Rosepath variations listed earlier. As you weave, patterns appear as if by *magic*.

Completed sampler (folded over) of plain weave, 3/1 twill, and rosepath with computer drawdowns.

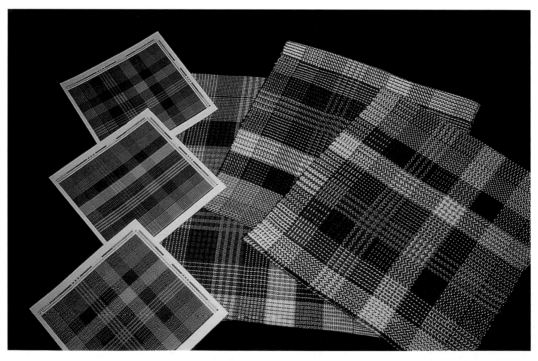

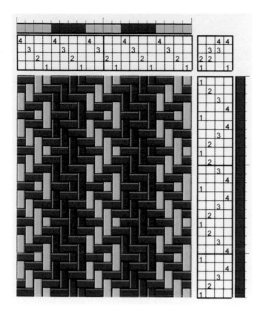

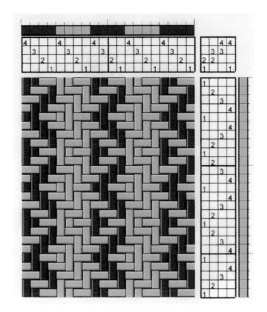

Select a simple vest pattern. Check pattern pieces before weaving for width and length. Calculate the amount needed for warp and weft. My fabric needed to be approximately 18" wide. The 5/2 cotton was sett at 16 epi (double in an 8 reed) equalling 288 threads plus four threads for doubling edge threads and floating selvedges (292 total).

The warp is four blue and four gold across, ending blue. Figuring vest requirements plus take-up, loom waste, and shrinkage, I tied on the previous warp and rolled 4 yards on the loom. This included 12" sampling, then tying on the front again to weave

1½ yards each fabric for the vest, half with gold weft and half with blue weft.

Wet-Finish: Wash in warm water with neutral soap, rinse well, block, hang until almost dry, and steam press. Cut the fabric and overedge to prevent unraveling. Rather than full seams, save inches by overlapping and stitching selvedges together at the center back. Rope trim accents the front and neck edges.

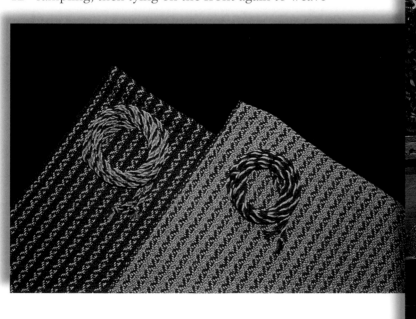

Rags to Riches

Sectional warping is the third classic method of warping. It is excellent for weaving very long warps.

A sectional warp beam is a warp beam separated into 1" or 2" sections by pegs or wires, with a tie-on cord in each section. A **section** on a sectional beam is the space between the pegs or wires.

A **tension box** evenly tensions a set of threads as they are rolled on in each section of a sectional warp beam. Directions should come with a new tension box. One advantage of warping

Jack loom set up for sectional weaving from Schacht Spindle Co.

with a sectional beam is that no paper or sticks are needed between each layer of threads.

The classic method of sectional warping uses spools from a **spool rack**. Each spool carries one thread that fills one thread of that section. For example, for a sett of 6 epi, you need 12 threads in each 2" section, which requires 12 spools filled with at least the length of that warp multiplied by the number of sections to fill with that thread. Each sectional beam can hold 80 yards or more, depending on the actual loom and thread size. An optional yardage counter keeps track of the length of the threads in each section as they are wound on so that threads in all sections come out the same length.

A spool rack and, on the bench, a yardage counter.

WEAVERS AROUND THE WORLD

In Thailand, Mrs. Viroy Nanthaphoom (right), Master Weaver, weaves silk ikat threads that have been tied beforehand in specific patterns and dyed with indigo at Weaver Patricia Cheesman's Studio Naenna in the Chom Thong district of Chiang Mai. Sigrid Piroch (left), as American Cultural Specialist, was on a teaching tour sponsored by the U.S. State Department and U.S. Embassies in Thailand and Laos.

Rag Place Mats, Mug Rugs, and Shaker Rug Sampling

Rag rugs are frequently woven with carpet warp. These projects use 8/4 cotton carpet warp doubled, *two ends used as one*. For this modified method, you make a warp on a warping board for each 2" section of 12 doubled threads (24 threads total). Treat each two threads doubled as one thread throughout warping. At the final stage of warping, one set of two threads goes through each heddle and each reed dent in the beater on the loom.

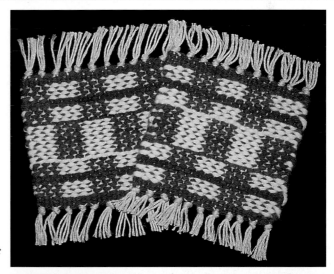

Double-face weave.

Sectional Warping

Make seven mini-warps, one for each section in this color order: dark, medium, light, medium, light, medium, dark. Add two extra threads at the edge, the dark color, one for each side as floating selvedges. Chain and store these mini-warps on lease sticks until warping begins. You can work with these mini-warps in the lease sticks or use your fingers to keep the cross, threads in order, and carry them to the tension box.

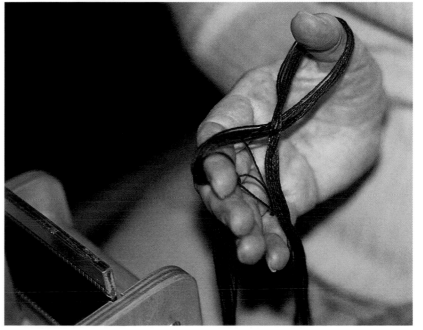

You can use your fingers to keep the cross.

TENSION BOX

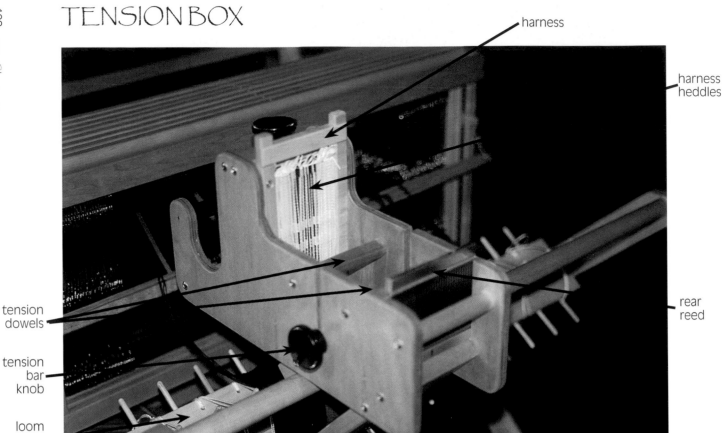

harness

harness heddles

tension dowels

tension bar knob

loom sectional beam

rear reed

Tension box back (Schacht Spindle Co.).

harness

knob to adjust pivoting reed

front dowel

pivoting front reed

rear reed

tension dowels

tension bar knob

loom back beam

Tension box front and side (Schacht Spindle Co.).

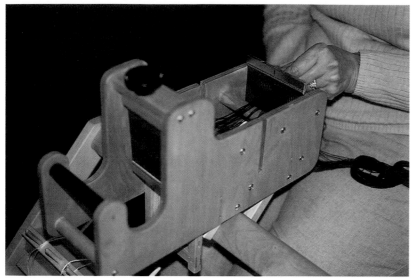

1. Center and thread the cut ends of the mini-warp evenly across through the rear reed.

2. From the side facing the back of the tension box, center the mini-warp through the harness heddles using a threading hook.

3. At the same time from the side facing the front of the tension box, thread the pivoting front reed.

From here, refer to labels in the tension box photos on the pervious page. Place the tension box on the back beam of the loom across from the first section to be filled. Remove the tension bar. Place the tension box **harness** in the center position (not up or down). *Working from the back* of the tension box, center and thread the cut ends of the mini-warp evenly across through the **rear reed**. Next place these threads over both **tension dowels**.

The first thread goes *through* a heddle on the harness and through one or more dents in the reed. The next thread goes *between* that heddle and the next heddle and again through the reed. Repeat across.

Adjust the pivot so the threads occupy the full 2" across the **front dowel**. This will fill the 2" space on the beam evenly. Make a snitch knot by first tying an overhand knot of the ends of the group of threads, then make a lark's head knot of the cord from that section and slip the overhand knot through the loop at the end.

Replace the tension bar on the tension box. With the loom **crank**, wind on the cord and then the threads. The knot should fall about the middle of the section. Continue to roll on these threads, carefully adjusting the pivot angle as needed. Stop while the threads are still through the box, the ends about 6" from the back reed. Trim these ends evenly and slip knot.

Raise the tension box harness to create the first part of the cross and insert a holding thread. Lower this harness for the second shed of the cross and place the holding thread through it as well. Reposition the harness in the center position. Tie holding cord ends together.

1. Make a snitch knot of the ends from the box and the tie-on cord in that section of the back beam.

2. The hand in this photo, partially hidden behind the box, is cranking.

3. Raise the tension box harness. Place holding thread through the shed.

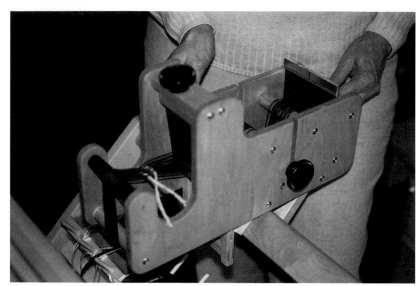

4. Tie, holding the cord ends together.

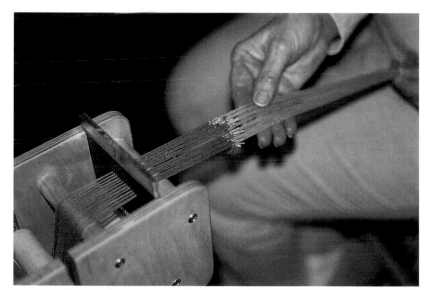

5. Tie on the next mini-warp, thread to thread.

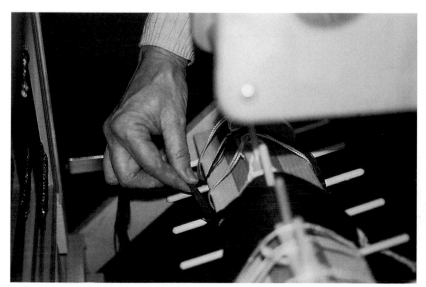

6. After rolling on the next mini-warp, anchor the threads around the peg.

Release the slip knot at the back of the tension box. Tie on the next mini-warp to the previous mini-warp, thread to thread. Wind the threads through the box onto the beam until the knots are through the box with 6 inches to spare at the front. Cut out the knots by cutting on either side of the knots straight across. Either slip knot the ends of the wound warp and anchor these threads on the sectional beam around a peg, or use painter's masking tape to catch the ends in order to be picked up later to thread in this order. Make an overhand knot of the new mini-warp ends at the front of the box.

Move the tension box so it is centered over the next section. Make a snitch knot by slipping these overhand-knotted threads through a lark's head knot made of the cord from the sectional beam in the new section. Wind and repeat as before.

Once all the sections are filled, from the lease sticks, pick up the cross from each section and tie the lease sticks behind the heddles on the loom. Now proceed by threading the heddles and reed, warping "back to front" as in Chapter 9.

7. Roll on the warp, then thread the heddles and the reed.

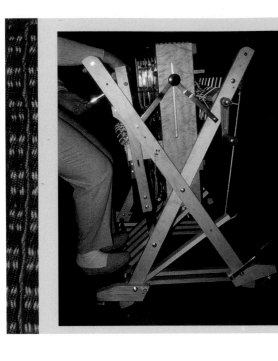

Hint

The loom shown is an X-frame—you see the X from the side. To make it easier to thread an X-frame loom, fold it part of the way up until the heddles and reed are at a working height.

NOTE: Thread every other dent of a 12 reed for a sett of 6 epi, or every dent in a 6. (Check the *Sett Chart* on page 43 for more alternatives.) Three colors of warp set off this design, but one color would also work, since the color-and-weave effect is primarily the result of the rotation of the weft rag colors.

PROJECT LAYOUT:

Project	4 rag place mats and 4 mug rugs; Shaker rug sampling
Equipment	4-shaft loom for mats and mug rugs; 2- or 4-shaft loom for Shaker sample; rag shuttle optional
Structure	Double-face weave with rags for mats and mug rugs; plain weave with Shaker twisted wefts—no tabby used between rag picks
Yarns and colors	Warp: 8/4 cotton carpet warp at 1680 yd./lb.—each thread used double—in 3 colors: dark, medium, and light. Weft rags: dark, medium, and light (accent) colors/patterns—rip 1½" for mats and 1" for mug rugs; dark and light for Shaker twist samples. If new fabric is used: 2 yards of 45" wide cotton for each of the 3 colors for the entire project.
Sett	Each end is doubled and used as one end—1 doubled per dent in a 6 reed or 1 doubled every other dent in a 12 reed
Width in reed	Approximately 14" for mats, 4" for mug rugs
Make warp	Mats: 90 working ends, each one a doubled thread of two actual threads = 180 total threads; this includes seven 2" sections with 12 doubled threads each = 84 (168) + 2 doubled selvedges each side = 88 (176) plus one floating selvedge each side made up of two threads each = 90. Mug rugs: drop all but the center 36 threads (72 total) for mug rugs. Shaker: use same warp
Plain Weft	Rags as indicated

Make the warp two threads at a time since two threads are used as one working thread throughout the warping and weaving. Double-face weave (two blocks on 4 shafts) is reversible. Mug rugs are woven "on opposites" using shafts 1-2 and then 3-4. Sample the Shaker twists or use this weave for an entire project.

Blocks: The term "block" in weaving is used in various ways. With this project, "threading Blocks A and B" refers to *threading* units, 4-3-1 and 4-3-2 that repeat. The color placement produces an area that looks like a block. Blocks A, B, C, and D are each *treadled* the same so they are not different in structure, only the order in which the colored rags are thrown alters their appearance.

Colors: This project uses three colors for the *warp*: dark blue at the sides, medium blue, and tan alternate across. The *weft* uses the same three hues, but ripped into rags.

Prepare the Rags: A rag is any cloth ripped into strips, new or used. You can prepare rags for weaving on the grain or on the bias, as separate strips, or continuous. I opted to rip on the grain, 1½" wide for the mats and 1" for the mug rugs. I trimmed the rags on a slant and overlapped them in the shed. You can also slit the end and loop them through (top) or sew them together at right angles, trimming the triangle (bottom).

Weave place mats according to the draft. Weave heading with dark carpet warp in plain weave for eight picks, weave rags according to the color bars for Block A, B, C, D, repeat until about 15" is woven, and weave another heading. A **temple** is useful to keep the warp from drawing in too much. Rag shuttles, rug shuttles, and ski shuttles work well, but at this width, so does a stick shuttle.

Fabric, rags, and yarns used for this project.

Connect rags in various ways.

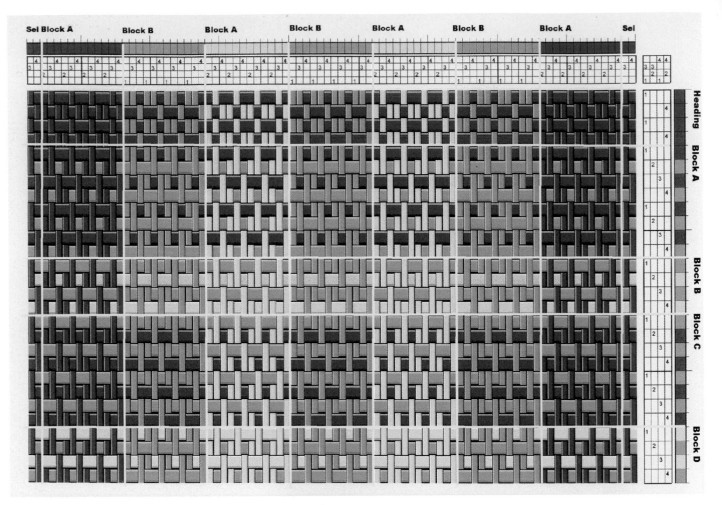

	Sel	Block A		Block B		Block A		Block B		Block A		Block B		Block A		Sel

Draft for place mats.

Use a temple to keep the warp from drawing in too much.

Use a heavy beat. The bigger and heavier the floor loom, the easier it is to beat hard. Picks should be so tightly woven that you can't budge the rags with your fingers. If you hold a rag weaving up, no light should show through. Rags do not "turn the corner" at the selvedges as easily as yarns. For a better selvedge, pinch the rag as it turns and twist it so it lies properly in the next shed. These cotton rags have pattern on only one side, so each strip is folded in half, pattern out, so it is visible on both sides of the weaving. Use 3" spacers of cardboard cqualling 6" of unwoven warp between each mat for fringes. Off-loom, tie an overhand knot, three for each color block, then braid these three together, ending with a double thread wrapped around the ends.

Weave mug rugs on this warp after the mats are cut off; drop 24 threads each side so the three center blocks remain threaded. Convert the last set of threads on each side to floating selvedges. Untie and re-tie the treadles for weaving on opposite sheds 1-2 (treadle 1) and 3-4 (treadle 2). Using 1" rags, weave four picks blue, two tan, two blue, three tan, three blue, four tan, and reverse.

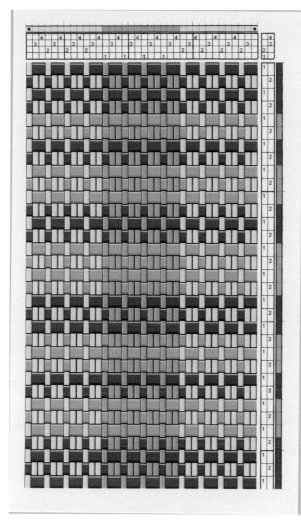

Draft for mug rugs.

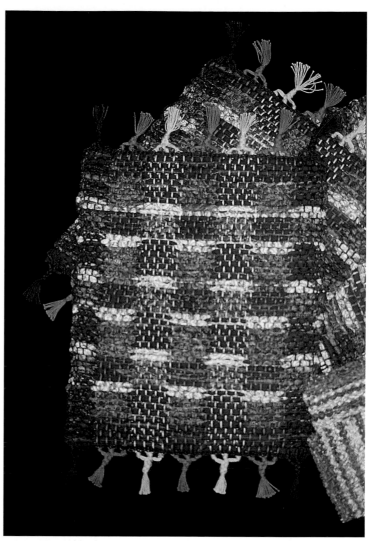

The finished place mats.

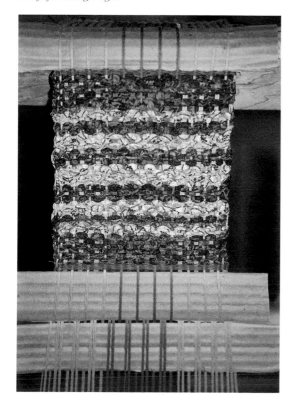

Corrugated cardboard inserts separate one mug rug from the next.

Off-loom, work these ends back into the fabric on the reverse with a crochet hook for a smooth edge finish.

Shaker Rug Sampling

You only need two plain weave sheds and two contrasting rags to create these interesting effects.

Vary the twist direction and use a single rag at intervals to separate the designs. One sample, in the photo (right), shows two rags (light and dark) twisted in one direction in one shed; in the next shed these rags are twisted the opposite direction, switching direction again in the next shed for a zigzag effect. "Arrowhead designs" form, as you twist them in the shed, if you align the dark areas. Four rows of these twists are followed by two rows using a single rag.

Twist two rag strips, one light and one dark, in the shed.

Beat firmly and repeat.

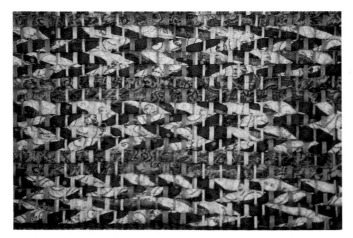

This sample shows two rags (light and dark) twisted in one direction in one shed, alternating four times; then one color for two rows.

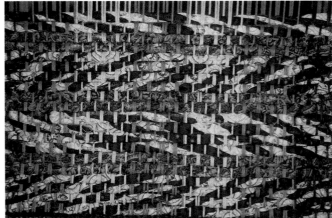

This sample shows rags twisted in one direction for four picks, two picks of a single color, then four picks of rags twisted in the other direction. Experiment with your own designs.

Samplers are a good way to try out various rug techniques. A series of rug samplers shows dozens of different techniques and end-finishes.

Rya is a method of knotting yarns or rags around the warp, one at a time. An efficient shuttle method to weave rya, called "double corduroy," was developed by Peter Collingwood. Below is a "Patriotic Rug" on the loom in his technique using rags.

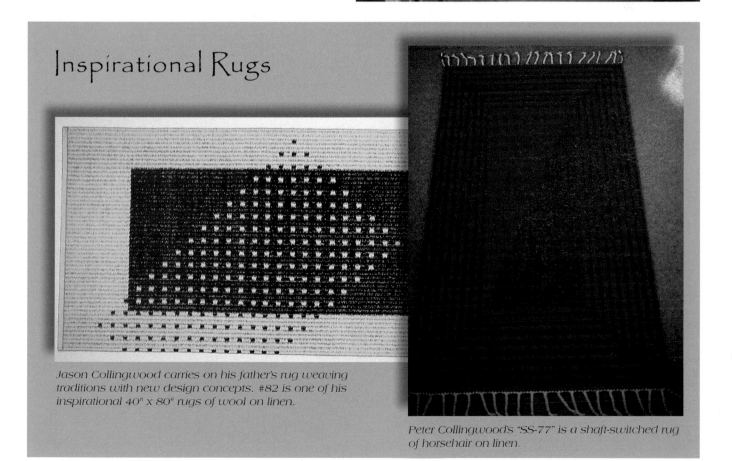

Inspirational Rugs

Jason Collingwood carries on his father's rug weaving traditions with new design concepts. #82 is one of his inspirational 40" x 80" rugs of wool on linen.

Peter Collingwood's "SS-77" is a shaft-switched rug of horsehair on linen.

12 Follow Your Star

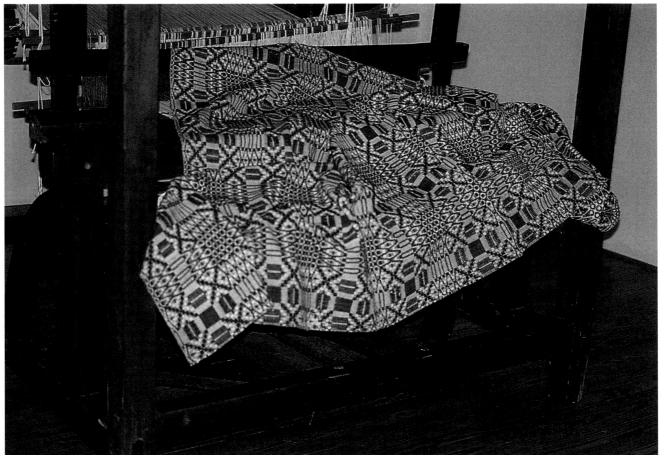

Historic overshot coverlet woven on four shafts in the early 1800s on a pattern loom available to home weavers, in a pattern called "Turtle Back."

Overshot is a weave that has long been a favorite of new weavers. Popular in nineteenth century America for handwoven coverlets, it has never lost its appeal. Overshot patterns may look complex, but can be woven on any loom with only four shafts. The name *overshot* describes the process—one *shot* (pick or shuttle throw) of the weft *shoots* over some warp threads to form pattern. When this pattern weft skips over the same series of threads a number of times in sequence, a *block* is woven on the face of the fabric. (Like other supplemental weft weaves, alternating picks of tabby form the ground.) Four shafts form four blocks, each

woven using a pair of shafts. Threads in a weaving draft are numbered; blocks are alphabetical. The four overshot blocks are Block A, Block B, Block C, and Block D. The fabric is single layer and reversible; the pattern on one side is the reverse of the other.

Because overshot was traditionally woven on counterbalance looms in America and since traditional overshot drafting comes from that tradition, it makes sense to draft it this way. For this exercise only, overshot is drafted as a *weft drawdown* for a *counterbalance loom*. When you weave Block A = 1 plus 2 on a counterbalance loom, the threads on these shafts sink; consequently the pattern weft shoots over

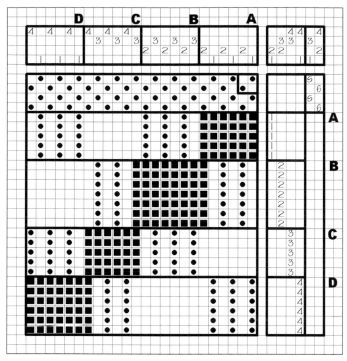

This overshot draft on four shafts shows the four pattern blocks that develop in threading and treadling, A through D. Block A is 1 plus 2 tied to treadle 1; Block B is 2 plus 3, treadle 2; Block C is 3 plus 4, treadle 3; and Block D is 4 plus 1, treadle 4.

all threads on the first and second shafts.

Two tabby treadles are tied up as 1 plus 3 and 2 plus 4, shown weaving a heading at the top of the drawdown. Drafts generally do not include tabby since the focus is on the pattern—weavers know to weave it in alternately with the pattern picks.

The solid dark areas are pattern wefts that skip over a series of warps, creating the pattern blocks on the face (these are all white areas on the back). The white areas are pattern wefts that skip under a series of warps on the face (these form pattern blocks on the back). Vertical dots, called *half-tones*, are pattern wefts that are a visual mix of both (seen on both sides).

Overshot is a close relative of twill, so threading and treadling must be kept in "twill order" (see Chapter 10). With twill, each successive *pick* overlaps and moves diagonally; with traditional overshot, each successive *block* overlaps and moves diagonally. The threading always alternates odd and even shafts.

In the draft above, blocks can be drafted and woven with six picks per block, or woven with any number to square on finishing, but traditionally the treadling is developed from the threading. Blocks A to D in this draft are made up of 5, 7, 5, and 6 picks respectively, so each block *drafts* out square. The

actual number of picks in any given block varies in overshot because the treadling is developed from the threading and there is an overlapping thread where one block intersects with another block at the corner.

In the *threading area* of this overshot draft illustration (left), each block is threaded with *six* threads, so the weft skips over six or more warp threads.

Let's look at an historic overshot pattern known as "Four Spears." The rich patterning is created by three visually different blocks that tantalize us all at the same time on the face of the cloth: (1) solid blocks of red or green; (2) all-white areas; and (3) half-tone blocks mixing white with red or green. No half-tone blocks are visible in the all-white pillow. The pattern has disappeared and has become texture.

The green pillow is sewn face up "star fashion" (defined later). The red pillow and green afghan show the other side of the cloth, including the motifs that form the four spears.

All overshot drafts are made up of blocks that form motifs. In *traditional* overshot, all blocks on the diagonal are square; other blocks are either square or rectangular. Most overshot drafts have two motifs, each made up of two blocks. Typically, each block is drafted with an even number of threads in each block *except* at the center of a motif—this block has an odd number of threads to balance the pattern on both sides. It is known as the *turning* or *reversing block*.

"Four Spears" patterned pillows and afghan.

A red star is located over the turning block at the center of each motif—one motif is repeated to balance the pattern. (Should you come across an overshot draft with all even blocks, add or subtract one thread in each turning block.)

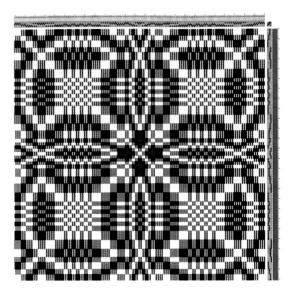

Draft of the back of this same pattern showing the "four spears" at the center (colored in red).

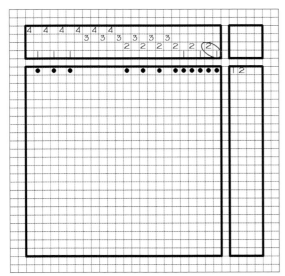

Begin to draft the block "as drawn in."

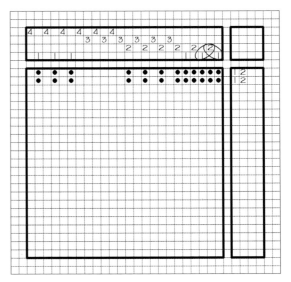

Draft the second line.

This overshot pattern above is "star fashion," which you can see by the large red "X" drawn on top. When drafted traditionally "as drawn in," an "X" forms in some patterns as a 45-degree unbroken line drawn corner to corner in both directions over the pattern blocks. The line on the face, as here, covers only dark pattern blocks.

"Rose fashion" is a treadling conversion from "star fashion." The result is a rounded pattern. To convert from star fashion to rose fashion, the two blocks in each motif switch places. So if one motif is made up of blocks ABA, these will now be woven BAB; if the second motif is made up of blocks DCD, then it is woven CDC. This is another way to weave a wonderful

traditional pattern on the same threading. Although subtle, in rose fashion, a 45 degree unbroken diagonal line covers only half-tone blocks. Not all overshot patterns are star fashion or rose fashion.

Drafting Overshot

One of the most confusing things for many handweavers is to understand the traditional method of developing the treadling for an overshot threading, a method called **"as drawn in"** or **"tromp as writ."**

Try this time-honored method by using the same four-block draft. To draft the first block "as drawn in," begin with the first pick. Working right to left, circle the first two threads in the threading draft (1-2)

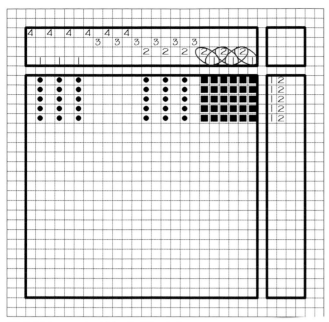

The first overshot block, Block A.

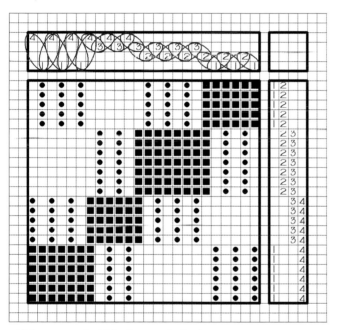

All four overshot blocks are drafted.

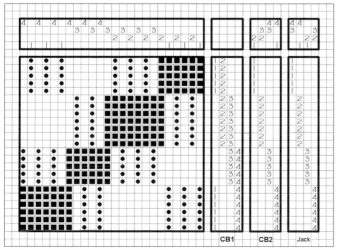

The treadling is converted to a tie-up, and from counterbalance to jack.

and write 1-2 in the first line of the treadling draft. Leave the tie-up blank for now. Place a dot below each 1 and 2 in the drawdown as shown.

Next, circle *the last thread previously circled* plus *the next*, 2-1, and write this 1-2 in the second line of threading draft. Fill in the dots as before.

The illustration at left shows five 1-2's circled. These five make up the first overshot block = Block A. Any time two or more dots come together *horizontally*, fill them in as a solid, making it easier to see the pattern blocks. (In overshot, *vertical* dots always remain dots.)

Continue circling all block combinations and listing them in order in the treadling. Now all four overshot blocks are drafted.

If you weave on a table loom, you can follow the draft without filling in the tie-up area, but since most table looms are jack looms, you need to "weave the blanks." That is, where there is a 1-2 in the treadling, pull 3 and 4 to activate that shed. Where there is 2-3, pull 1-4; 3-4 becomes 1-4 and 1-4 becomes 2-3. If you forget to convert, the pattern will be on the underside.

If you have a loom with treadles, convert the treadling to more than one shaft per treadle, in accordance with the type of loom you have. The left treadling column in the illustration (bottom left) is marked "CB1" (for counterbalance step 1); this matches the previous draft. To convert this counterbalance treadling to its counterbalance tie-up, see the center column marked "CB2" (for counterbalance step 2). The four block combinations generated in the treadling have been moved to the tie-up: the 1-2 in the treadling area now becomes treadle 1, the 1-2 moves to the tie-up squares above it. Repeat for the other three treadles and the other three tie-up combinations. If you have a counterbalance loom, you are ready to weave "as drawn in." If you have a jack loom, simply weave the blanks in the CB tie-up instead. Or, more formally, fill in the blanks with the numbers for the jack loom—leave the CB loom tie-ups blank. If you have a countermarch loom, fill in the jack numbers with Os and the jack blanks with Xs.

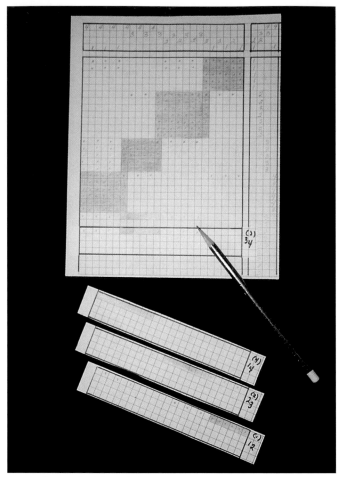

A set of overshot templates.

Overshot patterns can be quite large, so **templates** will help you drawdown overshot or any other pattern faster and more accurately by hand. Because overshot has four pattern blocks, make four templates. Cut each template of the same graph paper, about four squares down and a little wider than the width of the drawdown. Make a strong line at each side where the drawdown begins and ends, then copy one pick of the solid and dotted blocks across for each of the four blocks on each template. Mark each one 1-2, 2-3, 3-4, or 4-1 accordingly. Complete the drawdown.

Treadled as Threaded: In many weaves, for example huck lace (Chapter 13, page 135), a threading turned 90 degrees is the appropriate treadling for that structure. Perhaps this accounts for part of the confusion with overshot which, as discussed, has its own special method of developing the treadling blocks. What will happen if you take the threading for "Four Spears" and copy it sideways for the treadling with the same tie-up? Since the overshot threading is in twill order, the tie-up is a 2/2 twill, the treadling now is also in twill order—the fabric is twill. Each twill pick moves one thread on a diagonal, forward or back, just as in circle drafting (Chapter 8). The result is always a smaller pattern with short floats. I call this "treadled as threaded;" in this case, it is also "treadled as twill." These are ideal for weaving as miniature patterns.

Weaving Overshot

Traditionally in overshot, tabby is woven with the same weight yarn as the warp, or half as fine—often both of cotton, the pattern weft heavier and softer than the warp—frequently of wool. Any soft pattern yarn covers the ground well so the blocks are seen as a unit.

Sampling for sett for each overshot pattern is of critical importance, especially since overshot patterns are traditionally woven square. Patterns with long float blocks beat in more readily than those with mostly short floats. As with other weavings, sett and beat varies with width in the reed. A wider warp requires a harder beat for the same number of picks per inch, so a more open sett is often required for a project compared to a narrow sample.

"Four Spears" front and back, "treadled as threaded."

WEAVERS AROUND THE WORLD

The Salvi brothers precisely adjust each thread. Just 15 years ago, there were 15 family members working on one patola, but now only four still weave. Unless they take on apprentices, this specialized weaving may disappear.

The Salvi brothers are famous for weaving silk patola cloth in double ikat in Patan, India. They tie and dye all vertical and horizontal threads, then weave so the design fits together in both directions.

The Estes Sampler is woven of 70/2 linen warp sett at 45 epi, cotton-covered sewing thread tabby, 36/2 Finnish wool pattern weft, using patterns from the book, *Miniature Overshot Patterns for Handweaving.* There are two threading repeats of each pattern in the Estes Sampler of traditional white warp and white tabby with blue pattern. Fifteen patterns similar in size were threaded across with a few green threads in twill order between to separate them. Each was woven "as drawn in," the first two once and the others twice, with a few green threads of treadled twill between each block of pattern. "Maltese cross" is a classic variation.

Just fifteen patterns threaded and woven create (15 x 15) 225 designs on one side. Since the other side looks so different, the number doubles to 450. One overshot repeat usually has two motifs that work together, two blocks each; the larger one is sometimes called a **table** and the smaller one a **connecting unit**.

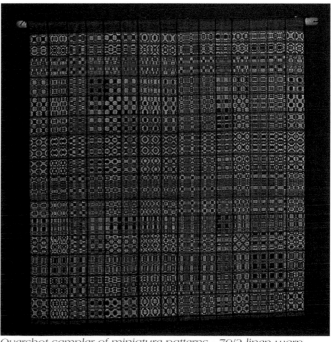

Overshot sampler of miniature patterns—70/2 linen warp, 36/2 wool, sewing thread tabby.

Detail of the Estes Sampler's two repeats of one unbalanced pattern.

The Estes Sampler: table. connecting unit. table.

Take the table from one pattern and the connecting unit from another to create a new pattern. Enlarge or reduce any motif(s). Introduce more colors and you have almost unlimited pattern possibilities from just one sampler. Samplers are great learning aids and create an entire library of patterns quickly. As overshot is woven, patterns appear out of the warp as if by *magic!*

Overshot usually needs an extra half pattern to create a visual balance. In this sampler, the patterns are purposefully repeated twice, but not balanced so as to leave the focal point undecided. There are two threading repeats for each pattern: a connecting unit and table threaded/woven twice, but not to balance.

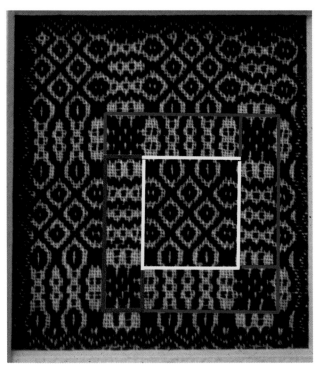

The Estes Sampler (above) with table outlined in yellow, one connecting unit in red, others around the table in green.

The Estes Sampler: connecting unit, table, connecting unit.

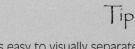

Tip

It's easy to visually separate patterns by using cardboard cut at right angles as a tool—make a set out of matting from old picture frames, as here.

Tyler first used a regal lion as his trademark.

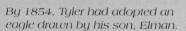

By 1854, Tyler had adopted an eagle drawn by his son, Elman.

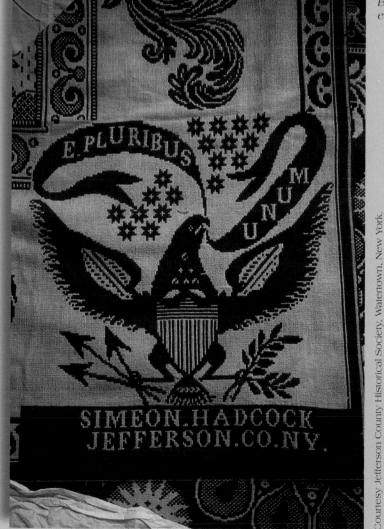

Harry Tyler (ca 1801-1858) was one of many professional handweavers in America who wove complex designs into coverlets on a jacquard loom using complex structures, such as these in doubleweave with two integrated layers. The yarns for these coverlets were likely dyed by his family—indigo for blue (Mary Hatch coverlet, above) and cochineal for red (Simeon Hadcock "E Pluribus Unum" coverlet, left).

13 Fabric Analysis is Fun

Kente cloth is woven as narrow strips in Ghana, Africa, then sewn together for larger weavings (collection of Emily Cline).

How do you weave a textile when there is no draft? There *is* a simple method to generate a full draft from a textile. Fabric analysis should be a basic tool in every weaver's bag of essentials.

Every fabric tells a story. When examined closely, a fabric gives clues to its nature and history. Antique textiles are some of the most exciting textiles to analyze.

Recently I discovered a set of antique towels in a shop, priced at only 25 cents each. Handwoven of fine linen, they are fringed and nicely hemstitched. Their red embroidered initials are typical of nineteenth century family linens. I wanted to analyze the towel pattern and structure, generate the draft, and weave replicas.

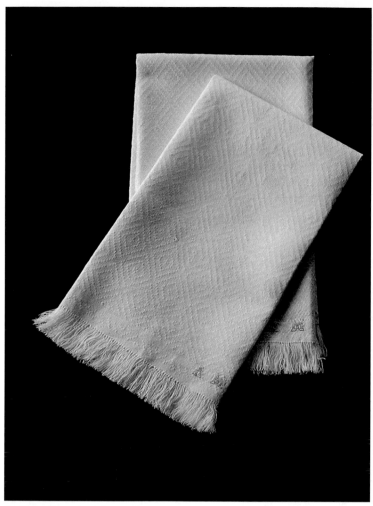

Antique linen hand towels.

Detail of one towel. Note initials, main and border patterns, hemstitching, and fringe.

Analysis tools: graph paper, lighted magnifying glass on a hands-free stand, hand-held magnifier, pick glasses (linen testers) which are strong mini-magnifiers, pencil and eraser, ruler, scissors, tweezers, picker (for separating threads to better see them), silk pins, pin cushion, needle, and thread

Thread-by-thread analysis is a lot easier with a helper, who need not be a weaver. One person analyzes while the other records information. Threads in these towels are so white and fine it is difficult to see and document their interlacement alone. Besides, it's more fun with someone else.

To do analysis, gather equipment and get comfortable. Sit where lighting is good, with your back straight, and elbows bent no more than 90 degrees. Either look through a hands-free magnifying glass at the fabric on a table, or use a hand-held magnifier with one hand, the fabric wrapped over your index finger in the other. With a more open weave, you may view the fabric best on a light table.

Recording Basic Information

Every fabric has much to tell if you look closely and collect the relevant facts: fibers, preparation, spinning, colors, weaving, and finishing. As you work, take notes and make sketches in a notebook.

1 Measure the item. Measure the width and length of the article in inches (used here) or centimeters—most pick glasses measure both. This towel is 22" wide by 26" long (excluding 1" fringe).

2 Record the characteristics of the fibers and yarns. Identify the fibers if you can. In an antique textile, cotton fibers are usually off-white and short, flax fibers are off-white to gray to yellow and much longer than cotton. Wool fibers are often long and hairy, etc. If the characteristics are not obvious, laboratory methods include burning, chemicals, and/or using an

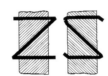

Threads "Z" and "S" plied.

electron microscope.

Threads in the towel in the photo are "Z" plied slightly uneven; because they are old, that tells me they may be handspun or early millspun. They are very white, so I document they are bleached. This can be a result of exposure to sun, dew, chemicals, or repeated washings.

3 Record fabric characteristics. What is your general reaction to the fabric? What is its purpose? How is it unique? How do you think it was finished? These towels are crisp and light of plied linen threads, washed to bring out the pattern, the little floats perfect for their use as toweling.

4 Determine the number of fabric layers. This fabric is single layer, the bottom threads the reverse of the top threads; all weft threads move through one set of warp threads. If in doubt, check to see if any threads keep to just one side of the fabric. If so, there are two surfaces to analyze.

5 Count warp and weft. Count epi (warps) and ppi (wefts), under magnification if necessary. This textile is 65 epi and 65 ppi, a very fine and perfectly balanced 50/50 weave. The handwork is exquisite.

6 Distinguish warp from weft. These towels have selvedges and fringe; the warp runs parallel to both.

Tips

1. Some threads are hard to see due to wear, climate, soiling, etc. If the fabric is matted or heavily felted, you may wish to shave fluff in a small section to better see the thread interlacement underneath. Holding some fabrics up to the light may help.

2. Most fabrics have a single layer. Doubleweaves, piqués, triple weaves, and other complex fabrics with two or more layers of cloth interlacing are tricky to analyze. Sidewinder drafts help document these. (If these names of structures are new to you, they await your discovery.) These fabrics require analysis of each layer, then establishing which threads interlace between the layers. Save for analysis after you're confident working with single-layered fabrics.

3. Sometimes you can tell the direction of the warp by the makeup or appearance of the fabric:
   (a) If one set of threads is two-ply and the other single, the two-ply is usually warp. (b) If one thread is softer in twist and/or thicker, it is usually weft. (c) If one is cotton and the other wool, cotton is almost always the warp. (d) Especially in antique fabrics, if linen is one direction and cotton the other, linen is usually the warp, since early mill cottons were not strong. (e) Most commercial twills move diagonally more in the warp direction than in the weft direction; the higher number is likely the warp. (f) In color-and-weave effect and supplementary-patterned fabrics, long skips are usually weft direction. (g) Warps are straighter than wefts since they are held under more tension during weaving as well as, if mill-produced, during commercial finishing. (h) Nap on commercially finished cloth is usually in the warp direction. Once you determine the direction of the warp, you know the direction of the weft.

7 Determine *front and back of the fabric*, although it is not always obvious. With a single-layer fabric, it doesn't matter from the standpoint of analysis because one side of the fabric will be the reverse of the other. (One side may, however, look better, obvious to all or a matter of opinion.) These towels are reversible, so either is the "right side." In this towel, initials tell the original intent.

8 Identify and mark what appears to be *one pattern repeat in both directions.* Be precise—place silk pins or contrasting thread *between* threads to mark where you begin and end your analysis. After one repeat is analyzed, do a second to confirm you have indeed documented the full repeat and there are no new warp/weft combinations—if so, the repeat is larger than you thought.

Record thread-by-thread weft analysis. This process is called "picking" because you literally pick through each thread and record how it interlaces. Use graph paper; mark each square where weft is on top of a warp and leave the square blank where warp is on top of a weft.

The towel with red stitches outlining one repeat of the four blocks and blue stitches outlining one repeat of the full pattern.

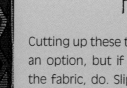

Hint

Cutting up these towels for analysis was not an option, but if you can cut a swatch of the fabric, do. Slip out one weft thread at a time at the top, read it off, and record it. (If for some reason the warp is easier to slip out, work in that direction.)

One thread is being "picked out" of a cut fabric.

WEAVERS AROUND THE WORLD

At a fashion show at the Handicraft Centre during a Lao Handicraft Exhibition in Veintiane, Laos, a model wears luxurious handwoven silks – a skirt and top – while holding a panel called a pha biang in her hands. Sponsored by the Ministry of Industry and Handicraft, businesses and village weavers work together to market their Lao products.

Analysis

NOTE: In the illustrations that follow, red outlines indicate the working area of the graph paper; red arrows indicate the direction for the current part of the analysis.

1 Decide who will pick through the fabric and call it out and who will record it on graph paper. To better see these threads, it is often helpful to use a pin to move them around.

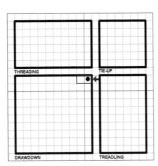

The first two analyzed weft threads are filled in the drawdown area of the draft.

2 Under magnification, begin in the drawdown area with the first weft thread at the marked upper right warp/weft intersection. If weft is on top, call out *up*. If it is not, call out *down*. This first weft thread in this example is over the warp thread, so it is *up*, documented as a *dot* in the upper right hand corner square of the drawdown. The next weft thread is under a warp thread, so it is *down*; that square is left *blank*. The first two analyzed *weft threads* are filled in the drawdown area of the draft.

3 Continue across horizontally until the first row is completed and then do the second row the same way. The first two *weft rows* are analyzed and filled in. Continue across until all weft rows are completed. The illustration shows the completed towel analysis for two pattern blocks.

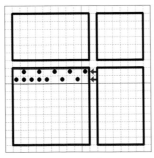

The first two weft rows are analyzed and filled in.

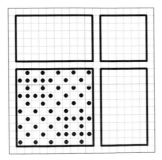

Completed towel analysis for two pattern blocks.

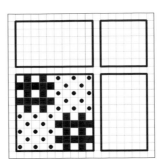

Two analyzed huck blocks, converted.

4 Convert the dots to solids where more than one warp or weft is adjacent, both horizontally and vertically. Conversion makes the lace motifs easier to see.

5 Now that the structure of the cloth is analyzed, the drawdown area filled in, you can generate the threading. Look at the first *vertical column* on the right in the drawdown area and mark 1 in the first square above it in the threading area. Now look at the next vertical column in the drawdown area; does this column have dots in the same vertical squares as the first? If it does, then put another 1 above in the threading area; if it does not, put a 2 on the second line of the second column in the threading area—2 is correct.

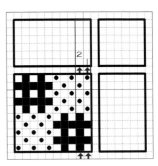

Begin to generate the threading.

Continue working to the left using the vertical drawdown rows to fill in the threading: for every column the same as 1, put another 1 above, for every 2, put a 2. For new combinations, put a 3 then 4. Remember, a dot and a solid both represent the same thing, a weft thread on top. (If you become confused, keep the dots and convert to solids later.)

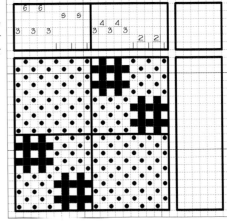

The threading generated for four blocks and six shafts.

Continue the analysis across as before. Two new shafts are discovered: 5 and 6. The threading is now complete for all four blocks on 6 shafts: 1-2-1-2-1, 3-4-3-4-3, 1-5-1-5-1, and 3-6-3-6-3.

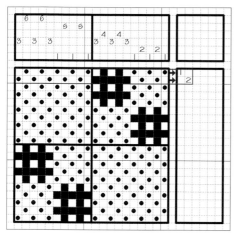

Begin to generate the treadling.

for each treadle, ask which dots/solids are directly under which threads: in the first row, for treadle 1, the numbers above the dots are 1, 4, and 6. So in the vertical tie-up column, exactly above the 1 in the tie-up area, put 1-4-6. The first treadle on the loom is tied to these three shafts.

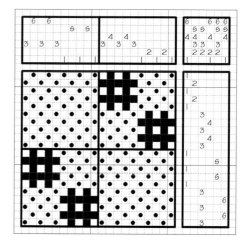

Complete structural draft for all four areas of the draft.

6 Now generate the treadling and tie-up. Look at the top *horizontal row* in the drawdown and mark 1 in the first square to the right in the treadling area. Now look at the next horizontal row in the drawdown; does this row have dots or solids in the same squares as the first? If yes, put a 1 on the second line in the second square to the right in the treadling area; if not, put a 2—2 is correct.

The second row has dots/solids in different squares than in the first row. These dots are directly under 2, 3, 4, and 5. Put these numbers in the tie-up area above the 2 in the treadling area.

Continue marking in the treadle and tie-up numbers. For each new combination, put a 3, then 4, then 5, then 6. Now you have the complete structural draft for the four huck blocks.

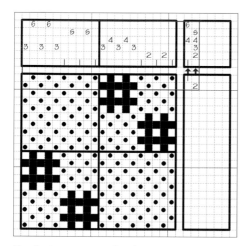

Begin to generate the tie-up.

As you list each treadle number in the treadle area, *horizontally* to the right of the drawdown area, put in the tie-up numbers *vertically* above it in the tie-up area. To know what numbers to put in the tie-up area

Some speculate that lacy weaves were the first structures woven after plain weave, created by mistakes while weaving plain weave cloth. Either weft skips across warp threads and/or warp skips across weft. Huckaback, nowadays shortened to huck, is structurally plain weave, but with pairs of threads skipping over three, five, or seven threads in one direction on one side and the opposite direction on the other. (This toweling skips over five.) Huck toweling, once commonly woven on home looms as well as sold by traveling merchants, has never lost its popularity.

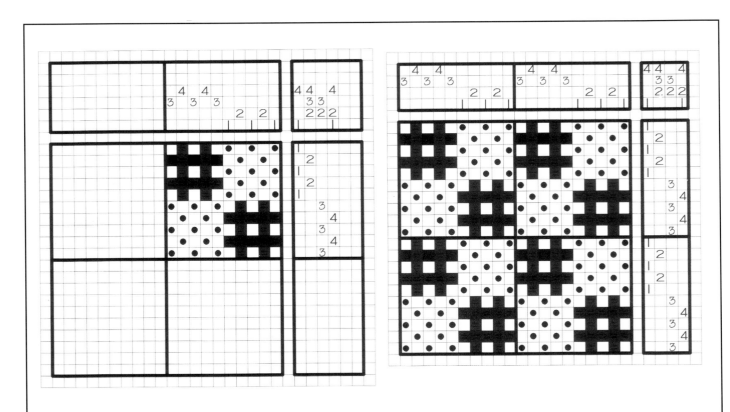

Draft converted to an interlacement drawdown.

You can convert this draft to an interlacement drawdown by placing horizontal lines in the squares with the dots/solids for weft and vertical lines in the blank squares for warp. To better visualize this, I've color coded the warp red-on-white and the weft black-on-gray. This draft is more "thread-like."

Which loom? When a treadle in this draft connects with the set of numbers above—say, treadle 1 to 1, 4, 6—these shafts drop on a counterbalance loom. (Instead of numbers in the tie-up, you can substitute Xs to indicate this.) If you have a jack loom, the shafts rise, so you need to re-write the tie-up opposite: the shafts in the blank squares are 2, 3, and 5. (You can put Os in these tie-up spaces instead of numbers.) In a countermarch loom, all numbers (Xs and Os) are used.

Roll back; use the 4-shaft alternative shown by the red square in the illustration to the left, above. Rewrite this and then generate a draft with two repeats for all-over huck lace. It's as simple as that.

The method presented is termed "weft analysis." Equally correct is a method called "warp analysis." The only difference between the two is that in weft analysis, the weft is marked on top with a dot or solid square; in warp analysis, the warp is marked on top. Use one or the other, but not both in the same draft.

WEAVERS AROUND THE WORLD

Weaving is a tradition of many Native American tribes. Navajo rugs span more than 300 years. One Navajo legend tells how Spider Woman taught Navajo women to weave. Spider Man told the people how to make a loom: cross poles were of sky and earth cord, warp sticks of sun's rays, heddles of rock crystal and sheet lightning, the beater a sun halo, and white shell the comb. Spindles for spinning were made of zigzag lightning with a whorl of coal, flash lightning with turquoise, sheet lightning with abalone shell, and rain with white shell.

Sarah Nantani is a well-known Navajo weaver who handspins wool for her rugs. Here she takes a completed rug off her upright Navajo loom.

A Navajo weaving in progress showing a raised outline technique, likely from the Coal Mine Mesa region of Arizona. (Weaver unknown.)

Weave a Towel Based on the Analysis

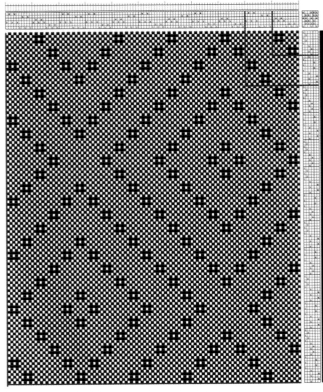

The draft for one pattern repeat of the analyzed fabric. Blue outer lines show the full draft, while red is one repeat of two blocks and then four blocks.

Compare the original antique towel (second from right) with the set of two replica hand towels of 5/2 cotton at 2100 yd./lb. (left two). This towel set is folded so you see each side, either of which can be the "right side," one with warp floats and the other weft floats towels. The guest towel (far right) is another replica with the same number of threads, but finer, using 20/2 cotton sett at 30 epi at 8,400 yd./lb.

The draft for the whole towel (right). To thread, use the draft (left), enlarging it if you need to see it better. Repeat the entire threading three times across, right to left. End with lace units 1-5-1-5-1 and 1-3-1-3-1 to balance.

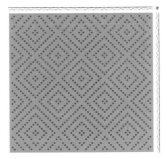

The threading, when turned sideways with this tie-up, becomes the treadling. (Example: Thread 1 becomes Treadle 1 tied to Tie-up 1 = 1, 4, 6.)

PROJECT LAYOUT:

Project	Huck Towels, 4-Block or 2-Block
Equipment	6-shaft loom or 4-shaft loom; one shuttle
Yarns	5/2 cotton at 2100 yd./lb., white warp and natural weft
Sett	15 epi, one thread per dent in a 15 dpi reed
Width in Reed	23"
Make a Warp	345 ends + 2 to double selvedges = 347 total x length calculated by the number of towels you wish to weave + fringe if desired, sampling, take-up and loom waste
Estimate Weft	the same yardage for weft as for warp since this is a 50/50 balanced weave

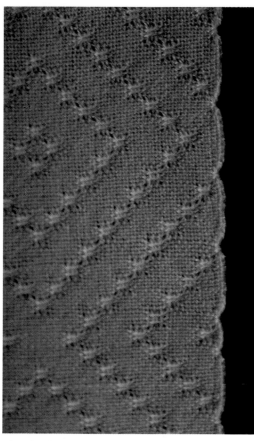

Hemstitching of the new towel. Note the vertical huck floats on this other side.

This huck threading produces natural scallops along the selvedges. Note the horizontal huck floats on this side.

NOTE: Huck is generally woven as a balanced 50/50 weave with warp and weft threads of the same weight and type in white and/or off-white as with these towels, but variations create interest.

Being able to analyze, modify, and re-create any textile provides an unlimited library of textiles for designing and adapting to your interests.

Historic Inspiration

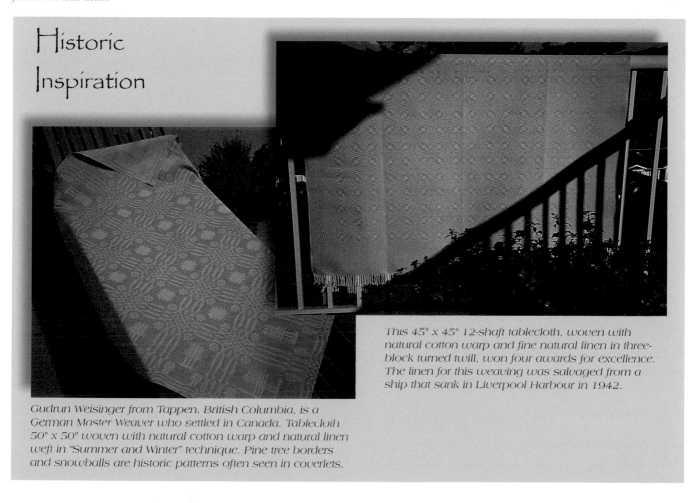

This 45" x 45" 12-shaft tablecloth, woven with natural cotton warp and fine natural linen in three-block turned twill, won four awards for excellence. The linen for this weaving was salvaged from a ship that sank in Liverpool Harbour in 1942.

Gudrun Weisinger from Tappen, British Columbia, is a German Master Weaver who settled in Canada. Tablecloth 50" x 50" woven with natural cotton warp and natural linen weft in "Summer and Winter" technique. Pine tree borders and snowballs are historic patterns often seen in coverlets.

24-shaft vest of silk squares; patterns from unpublished manuscripts circa early 1800s. The vest uses leftover silks. (Woven by Sigrid Piroch; sewn by Carol McGuire of Clarion, Pennsylvania; modeled by Christen Piroch.)

There's an old adage that "the one who dies with the most yarn wins." It's easy to accumulate lots of yarn and yarn ends that are leftovers/warpovers/weftovers from projects, specials from a favorite yarn store, and from guild sales. Even the smallest ends can be recycled. Every warp has loom waste that can be used for projects that do not need longer wefts: bands, inlay, tapestry, even stuffing sachets and pillows.

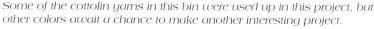

Some of the cottolin yarns in this bin were used up in this project, but other colors await a chance to make another interesting project.

Mixed Warps: What do you do with such a variety of leftovers? Uneven spacing and denting creates interesting texture in fabrics and can become an important part of designing. A heavier thread may only go through one dent while several finer threads fit through another. There is no tension problem weaving these if various types of threads are spaced all across the warp (but don't include linen, which doesn't stretch). Try wrapping various yarn sequences to see what you like.

Striped and Blended Warps: If you have lots of colors of one yarn or one color of assorted yarns, plan them together as a project. Sort them by yarn type, color, and/or size.

How can you plan an overall design when you don't know how much of each color you have? One way is to line up your yarns off the loom, in the order they can be used as warp on the loom, keeping in mind how colors work next to each other. Plan designs in related colors, or even a range of colors, from darkest to lightest. Twist yarns together to see how they look side by side. Squint to get a visual value "fix" on them—this works for yarns of the same color family, even different color families of the same intensity. Pure colors are difficult to use except as accent threads in a design. Muted colors blend nicely. Novelty yarns add interest.

Stripe a warp by changing from one color to another. Or blend these colors by warping one color for a section, alternating one-on-one with the next color for a section; repeat, begin and end with a darker single color.

Yarns you don't like tend not to be used. Take three such yarns/colors and twist or braid them—step back and you'll be surprised how they sort out their differences and create a new, more becoming color. One answer then is to warp by threes. Another is to warp so that three disparate threads are put together in a design.

Placemats, Napkins and Runner

Place mats, napkins, and runner.

Cottolin is a yarn blended of flax and cotton. Since the two fibers take dye differently, colors look heathery and work well together. Contrasting colors look tweedy, while colors of similar hue and intensity visually blend at this size to create new color effects. Cottolin wears well and becomes more comfortable with repeated washings, so it is ideal for clothing, as well as household items.

Project Plans: Make a warp of cottolin or other favorite yarns *twice as long as the project with a weaver's cross tied at both ends.* The warp is made twice as long, but only to the center with these colors. The top cross goes on the lease sticks to the right; the bottom cross goes on the lease sticks to the left. The colors reverse at the center. *Voilà!* A mirrored design by doubling over the warp.

Weave yardage for a series of coordinated fabrics: a runner 36" long, four place mats 18" long each, and four square napkins 14" each. These are approximate measurements off the loom and after wet-finishing, but before hemming. Fringe is not used. These plans are for a warp 12 yards long doubled over on the lease sticks for six yards. To make more or fewer items or to use different yarns, recalculate warp length and width with take-up, shrinkage, loom waste, and draw-in.

PROJECT LAYOUT:

Project	Place mats, napkins and runner
Weave Structure	Twill Blocks 1/3-3/1
Equipment	8-shaft loom, 1 shuttle
Yarns	22/2 Cottolin at 1750 yd./lb. on 250 yard tubes (or whatever you have left over)
Sett	24 epi, 2 per dent in a 12 reed
Width in reed	15"
Make warp	360 threads (120 sets of 3 threads) plus 1 set of 4 threads to balance the pattern = 364 threads plus 2 threads for floating selvedges if needed plus 2 threads to double edge threads = 368 threads x 12 yards; by threading both ends of the warp, you have 6 yards of 728 threads on the loom (plus 4 extras on each side = 8 total extras)
Estimate Weft	Approximately the same yardage in various colors

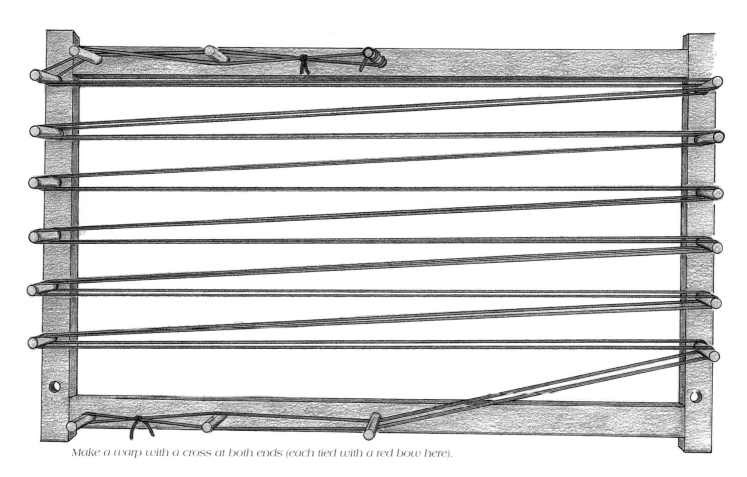

Make a warp with a cross at both ends (each tied with a red bow here).

Make a warp using three compatible colors at one time with a cross *at both ends*. (Note: pegs for crosses on my warping board are both on the left, so I end up with an extra half yard = 12½". If your warping board is 14 yards, you may wish to warp max for 7 yards on the loom.)

Since the amount of yarn left on each package differs in length, each yarn in each group of three will run out at a different time. The yarns/colors will continually change, blending and adding interest. As always, tie all knots for yarn changes at an end peg— top or bottom—on the warping board. The warp is half as long on the loom as on the warping board and twice as wide in the reed. Attach with lease sticks on the front beam.

Warp front to back or back to front. Thread 91 rounds of straight draw, 1 through 8, and repeat. Roll on all threads with the warp. With any extras you don't need, pull them off to the side for double-edge threads or use as floating selvedges or insurance in case of breakage.

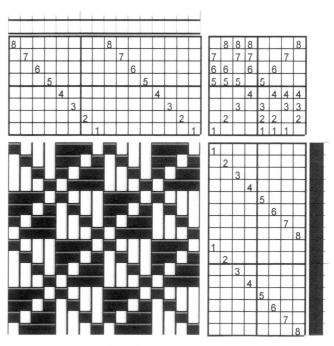

Draft of the two-block twill, two repeats.

Tip

Put any extra threads through the eyelets, mounted just above the heddle eyes on either side of the back castle, so they don't catch in the warp. Give them a tug each time you advance the warp so they're not caught in the warp.

Thread: Warp 1 through 8 following the threading draft. Thread/sley each group of three threads randomly in the reed/heddles. Avoid two of the same threads adjacent—this can create a visual line in the fabric. This tie-up is found in many historic draft books, but any twill tie-up for eight will work. (Don't have an 8-shaft loom? Thread 1 through 4 and try any 4-shaft twill tie-up.)

Weave: Since these items are all hemmed, there is no need for fringe or hemstitching. You can cut each piece off the loom as you weave it, but you would lose warp since you must tie back on. One way to reduce such warp loss is to *weave in a rod* with plain weave on either side, cut off and then lace this rod back on. And you can weave these projects as a continuous fabric, measuring and marking each item as you weave and weaving in a **cutting line** between each piece.

To weave a cutting line between items such as place mats, switch to a contrasting yarn; throw a pick in a plain weave shed but do not beat, repeat in the opposite plain weave shed and then two more picks without beating; use the beater to work the four picks slowly toward the fell of the fabric. This helps hold the threads together when they are cut apart later and evens tension. This is the same procedure as **spreading the warp**, used at the beginning of weaving.

Finishing: Lay flat, like in a bathtub and soak in warm water with pH-neutral soap. Allow at least an hour to absorb the water. Rinse in warm water, roll in towels to absorb some of the water, snap to block, hang until almost dry, and iron dry over a toweling to retain texture. Expect about eight percent shrinkage in the warp direction for take-up and wet-finishing, and less in the weft direction.

After washing finished projects, hang them until almost dry and iron over toweling to preserve the texture.

Caterpillar Bench Mat

Here is a quickie project to use up "weftovers." The loom is fast to set up in any width or length. As you are warping and weaving projects on other equipment, weave up your thrums and weftovers on this loom. Different sizes and/or types of yarns mixed at random make it even more interesting, or use 1/4" rag strips.

Known in Europe as far north as the Scandinavian countries, this idea was popular using yarns or rags. In this country during the 1930s, these were called "twice-woven rugs"—weave the chenille and then use the chenille as weft. Today, handwoven chenille yarn has a catchy name: caterpillars. This can also be used to trim garments and other fun stuff.

Woven bench mat.

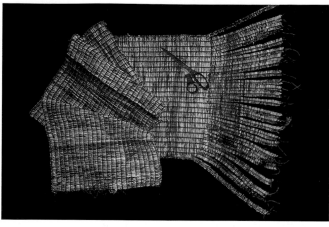

Cut all the way up between warp groups to create the caterpillars.

Old embroidery threads become the weftovers.

Lay flat or twist the caterpillars in the shed for different surface textures.

Make a warp, four yards or longer, of leftover fine threads in any color(s), such as 10/2 cotton, and thread them as a group. *Each thread in the set of eight threads goes through a separate heddle, but all eight go through one dent in the reed. Skip at least 6 dents and repeat across. (The longer the skip, the higher the pile in the finished fabric and the thicker the mat.)*

Thread the Warp:

(A) If you have a 2-shaft loom, thread 1-1-2-2 and repeat for eight threads total in each group; tie-up 1-2 alternating.

(B) On 3 shafts, thread 3-2-1-2 and repeat for eight threads; tie-up lifting each shaft once in the same order.

(C) For 4 shafts, thread 3-4-1-1-2-2-3-4, best because this threading locks in the threads; tie-up 1-3 and 2-4 weaving alternately.

Weave Weftovers: Beat hard. Weave until there is about a yard of warp left on the loom, cut off, and secure the warp ends on the loom with a slip knot. Tie the warp ends of the fabric at both ends (those that were dented together) to stabilize the weft. If you plan to wash the fabric, do it now. Cut between the warp groups.

Re-tie the warp on the front beam with the threads still spaced. To weave in the caterpillars, first tie the warp ends together and wind them on a stick shuttle. Beat hard. Lay the caterpillars flat in the shed to give the mat a velvety appearance shown here, or twist them in the shed for interesting random surface texture.

To estimate how much weft will fill the warp, weave at least three times in length the final area to fill. (Selvedge caterpillars are usually discarded.) Weave in plain weave. Trim the surface with scissors as needed. Wet-finishing is not needed. The mat, however, is a practical item and can be washed as necessary.

Triangle Fish

You can use up all the loom waste from essentially any warp by weaving a triangle on any standard loom.

Clip the right thread at the back rod, pull it out of the heddle and reed to the front, and weave it as weft right to left—plain weave sheds are simplest. Beat gently. Repeat from the right, weaving until you're out of threads. Twine, whipstitch, or hemstitch fringed sides to secure them; trim the fringes evenly.

These triangles make up into many items, including fish. Fold the triangle over into a smaller triangle, stuff, add eyes, sew sides together and you have a woven triangle, and not one thread on the loom wasted.

Triangle fish, "Go Fish Go." (Woven by Sigrid Piroch; hand-dyed by Connie E. Forneris. Thanks to Barbara Borgerd for the idea.)

A Bit of Whimsy

Holiday mobius scarves woven with natural rayon chenilles and metallics by Sigrid Piroch.

Photo by Sigrid Piroch.

Photo by Gordon Scale.

Meet "Bearella and the Family." Fabric handwoven of fine kid mohair using velvet technique by Sue Scale, bear designed and stitched by Jean Down, both of Carleton Place, Ontario, Canada. (From the Mississippi Bear Hug, Mississippi Blacksheep Gallery Inc.)

Postlude:
Circle of Love

I define myself in textile terms. My earliest memories are of textiles and a fascination with intricate patterns, beginning with my Great Aunt Dot, who taught me to crochet at age three. My mother was a painter and sculptor who did gorgeous single-strand silk embroideries as well as weaving; she taught me to sew at age five. Her mother and father were painters who met in the Minneapolis Museum of Art. My grandfather also was a composer whose works were premiered with the San Francisco Symphony. But his bread-and-butter was from his inventions—his factories turned out the first fully automated packaging machines in the world. My father was a conductor of symphony orchestras, providing live classical music in our circle of love.

My early passion for fibers and cloth, colors, and patterning set the stage for me to be a textile artist. It was when I discovered the tools of a spinner and weaver in the mid 1970s that I found my place. But it was my total commitment several years later to pushing the boundaries of weaving and sharing my discoveries through teaching that changed my life. Today, working through the context of conservation of our textile heritage, I thrive on the challenges of being on the cutting edge of the creation of new cloth in all its dimensions.

Sigrid wove this wrapping, entitled "Circle of Love" when her three children were quite small. It is still in use today by her three grandchildren, Theresa Marie, Joseph Nicholas, and Maura Anne Piroch.

Resources

Yarns

Halcyon Yarn
12 School St.
Bath, ME 04530
(800) 341-0282
www.halcyonyarn.com

JaggerSpun Yarn
Water St.
Springvale, ME 04050
(800) 225-8023
www.jaggeryarn.com

Lunatic Fringe
15009 Cromartie Rd.
Tallahassee, FL 32309
(800) 483-8749

Treenway Silks
501 Musgrave Rd.
Salt Spring Island, BC/Canada V8K 1V5
(888) 383-SILK
www.treenwaysilks.com

The Yarn Barn
918 Massachusetts Ave.
Lawrence, KS 66044
(800) 468-0035
www.yarnbarn-ks.com

Looms

AVL Looms
601 Orange St.
Chico, CA 95928
(800) 626-9615
www.avlusa.com

Baby Wolf floor loom:
Schacht Spindle Co. Inc.
6106 Ben Pl.
Boulder, CO 80301
(800) 228-2553
www.schachtspindle.com

Gentle Wovens
P.O. Box 3074
Escondido, CA 92033-3074
www.angelfire.com/ca5/gentlewovens/index.html

Harrisville Designs
Center Village
PO Box 806
Harrisville, NH 03450
(800) 338-9415
www.harrisville.com

LeClerc Looms
1573 Savoie
P.O. Box 4
Plessisville, QC G6L 2Y6
Canada
(819) 362-7207
www.leclerclooms.com

Macomber Looms
Beech Ridge Rd. P.O. Box 186
York, ME 03909
(207) 363-2808

Purrington Looms, LLC
P.O. Box 44
Scott Depot, WV 25560-0044
www.purringtonlooms.com

Loom Building Plans

Art McCathey
www.halfwaytree.com/looms

Weaving Software

Fiberworks PCW
www.fiberworks-pcw.com

PatternMakerPro
www.hobbyware.com

PatternWeaveSimulator
www.mhsoft.com

WeaveIt
www.weaveit.com

Other resources

Krause Publications
700 E. State St.
Iola, WI 54990-0001
(800) 258-0929
www.krause.com

Handweaver's Guild of America
www.weavespindye.org/

American Textile History Museum
491 Dufton St.
Lowell, MA 01854-4221
www.athm.org/athfame.htm

Ruth Stowe's Web site for a comprehensive list of fiber-related sites including Ron Parker's "list of lists" of fiber-related discussion groups
http://home.interlynx.net/~rstowe/weave.htm

Additional information and resources are available on the author's Web site: www.artsstudio.org

All hand-drawn illustrations are by Nancy L. Lewis and all computer-generated illustrations and photos are by Sigrid Piroch, unless otherwise credited.